The author joined the nursing profession a few short years after the National Health Service was launched, and when nursing was still an almost entirely female occupation. In the present era of political correctness and studied avoidance of sexual discrimination, male nurses are not exposed to the horrors which Mike Bolger recalls so amusingly in this book.

Born in Rotherham, Yorkshire, during the Second World War, Mike left school at fifteen, working mainly in catering until, in the swinging sixties, he decided to train as a nurse. A varied and colourful career then followed. He worked in hospitals and in the Ambulance Service receiving a top national award for saving the life of a child. He is now employed as a Nurse Specialist.

Mike is married with three grown up sons and lives in Sheffield in his beloved county of Yorkshire.

WHEN A MAN
CARRIES THE LAMP

Mike Bolger
RGN, RMN

When a Man Carries the Lamp

The Vanguard Press

A VANGUARD PAPERBACK
© Copyright 2000
Mike Bolger

A CIP catalogue record for this title is available from the British Library
ISBN 1 903489 00 8

Grateful acknowledgement is made to English National Board for
Nursing, Midwifery and Health Visiting for permission to reprint
excerpts taken from the 1963 examination paper.

Illustrations by
Tony Noon

*The Vanguard Press is an imprint of
Pegasus Elliot MacKenzie Publishers*

First Published in 2000

**The Vanguard Press
Sheraton House Castle Park
Cambridge England**

Printed & Bound in Great Britain

Dedication

To my wife
Judith

Acknowledgements

Thanks to:

Moria of 'ARIOMA' for help and assistance with the manuscript.

CHAPTER ONE
Dream Come True, or Horrible Nightmare?

"The lamp, man, adjust the bloody lamp, can't you?"

Halfway through an abdominal operation, the surgeon decided that the theatre light was positioned incorrectly. I grabbed hold of the big lamp, which hung directly above and shone down upon the operating table, and made a small adjustment.

"No, no, your casting a shadow – shine the damn thing into the wound can't you?"

Further efforts on my part only made the situation worse.

"Get out of my theatre"

"Look, can someone with a few more brains cells than a turnip lend a hand," bellowed the surgeon.

The anaesthetist rose from his seat at the head of the operating table. Slowly, he made for the lamp. Lightly, he touched it with his finger.

"Thank you, Robert." The surgeon was now at peace.

"Think nothing of it," murmured the anaesthetist, taking up his position once more.

From behind her mask, the theatre Sister glared at me. I felt it. I felt that glare more strongly than any looks of sympathy in the eyes of fellow nurses. All dignity, I judged, had been stripped from me during this small incident. For a long moment I considered myself a failure, a total nothing.

Two weeks into training for theatre nursing, I was now prompted into asking myself how the hell it was I was suffering a situation where, with a word, a curse, one could be so completely humiliated?

******

Eighteen months earlier, I had presented myself at the Victoria Royal, a hospital which, like its name, had the air of a large, middle-class hotel.

From an imposing, hilltop position, it overlooked a northern town characterised by large steelworks and coal pits. Together with most general medical services, it also provided a Casualty department, receiving and dealing with traumatic injuries around the clock. Across the town, I knew, was another hospital, specialising in diseases and conditions peculiar to women.

In the main building, I was directed by a curvaceous Staff Nurse. I stared after her as she swished out of sight.

"Naughty, naughty, you can get locked up for having

thoughts like that."

A hospital porter was grinning at me.

I laughed and, following my instructions, I started to walk in the direction of the Hospital Administrative Department.

"Why do you want to become a nurse?"

The matron's gaze was unflinching. The clock ticked impressively.

"Well...er...Matron, since leaving school I've had a few jobs, but none have really interested me. Working in a hospital, well, I think it might be something worthwhile, satisfying, if you know what I mean."

Silence.

"I know not many men are employed as nurses."

Silence.

"But I do think men have something to offer. Anyway,

I'd like to give it a try."

Silence.

"If, that is, you'll give me a chance."

Silence. That tick-tock-tick-tock, still counting away my life. Sweat ran down the back of my neck. I was a fool. I would be wise to get up and leave this room, now. Hurry, back into safe, familiar territory, where all expectations were clear and easy to fulfil. Now - run!

"Mm. But, Mr Bolger, there is a lot more to becoming a State Registered Nurse than that!" The pause allowed her words to sink in. "The life is not an easy one, especially for a man. As you say, we do not employ many males as nurses here, and we are highly selective about the ones we do."

The frill of the matron's cap shook a little as she turned the pages of my application form. "You have the necessary qualifications educationally, but you've certainly chopped and changed rather a lot since leaving school, haven't you?"

"That's true...er...Matron." I could only repeat what was, after all, the simple truth. "That's because I haven't yet found satisfaction in my work."

Did I catch a soft look, a warm look, in those clear, analytical eyes? Or was I just manufacturing approval?

However, the matron's words were cool, crisp and formal.

"Look, Mr Bolger, leave this with me, will you? Should we offer you a position, it would be subject to us obtaining satisfactory references for you and to you passing a medical examination."

I nodded. No further grilling! On the other hand, no further opportunity to impress.

"If accepted, and I say if, you will be notified in writing in due course."

The matron pressed a bell, which summoned a secretary, who ushered me from the room, gave me a date for a medical, then dispatched me, politely but efficiently, from the hospital.

My mother was peeling potatoes.

"How did you get on? Did you get the job?"

"I don't really know. I think..."

I nodded and went to fill the scuttle in the coal shed.

After some further form-filling and having attended the medical examination, I did indeed strive to forget about it.

The buff envelope fell on the mat. My appointment as a student nurse was confirmed. I was instructed to report in October, a month's time, to the School of Nursing.

Now I took the step which would burn my boats: that of informing my employers, a firm of cutlers, that I was leaving.

"You'll have to remember to keep your seams straight!"

My face burned.

"And your cap - you'll have to learn to keep that straight, and all!"

The remarks from work-mates were inevitable, and, I must confess, in their position, I would have made them myself. But they didn't help. I decided that the lads were envious of the probability that I would soon be surrounded by glamorous and vivacious females, and I defended my plans by rubbing that in.

Eventually, my father came round to accepting my ambition. A flood of stories about being a wartime sergeant radiographer in Burma was released. It's quite possible that his medical background had influenced my desire to nurse. Soon, far from his earlier opinion that the idea was crazy, Dad was asserting that I would soon be showing those hospital Sisters 'a thing or two'.

Privately, I was eaten up with doubt.

Would there be another man in the School?

How would I - me, my personality - be accepted?

Could I, in fact, cope with the life?

That it was a condition of employment that I 'live in' depressed me too.

On the eve of departure from home, I lay in bed, trying to sleep, but endlessly checking in my mind that I had packed all that would be required.

At last, lost in troubled sleep, I dreamed of running down long, dark corridors which led to nowhere but further long, dark corridors, the stink of disinfectant perpetually in my nostrils.

The Male Nurses' Home turned out to be a solidly built, detached house, to the rear of the hospital; it bore the name of Wellgate Mount.

A warm, friendly little woman answered the door.

"You'll be Mr Bolger," said Mrs Pottle. "I've been expecting you."

She unlocked the door to an upstairs room and handed me the key.

"A bit on the small side, I'm afraid - but if a bigger room falls free you can put in for it."

After offering a cup of tea, she chuckled reassuringly and clomped her way downstairs.

A dark-oak wardrobe and a small dressing table with a mirror were crammed into the room, with a single divan bed. I tested the mattress, finding it comfortable and modern (the springs in old-fashioned ones were always so noisy) - and was relieved to find I needn't stick my feet out of the window. I just fitted. As I sorted my clothes into drawers and hung up my jacket, I found I was singing.

Mrs Pottle (or Potty, as I later on learned to call her)

made tea the way I liked it.

"You'll meet my other gentlemen later," she said, extracting a particle of food that had been wedged under her dentures. "There's five in all: Mr Hessy, Mr Raja, and Mr Obasui - they're my black gentlemen - and then there's Mr Muller and Mr Graham, who are the same as you."

******

In solitude, I ate my evening meal in the hospital dining room. Small groups of nurses were talking in low voices. I decided against entering the communal lounge and returned to my new home.

There I found the full complement of inmates, and was invited to join them all in one of the larger bedrooms.

"Welcome to Bachelor House," said David Muller, introducing himself and the others.

It was clear that there was no prejudice between the ethnic groups present. Tony Hessy, an African, was to become one of my dearest friends. The tribal marks on his face, he told me, had been put there when he was an infant.

Already in his thirties, Ron Graham was the oldest.

"What's life like here, then?" I asked him.

"Oh, not bad really," he replied, smiling, "in spite of being ruled by a Petticoat Government."

This remark aroused my doubts once more. "What's the attitude to male nurses, then?"

"That you will find out for yourself," Ron said. "The majority are fine, but you get the odd one who thinks we have no right to be here. In fact," he continued, enlarging on what was clearly a source of anxiety, "only recently have we been allowed entrance to the hallowed halls of The Royal College of Nursing. Since its foundation in 1916, its doors have always been closed to us because of our gender. We still can't get a commission in the Armed

18

Forces, even though our equally qualified female colleagues get their pips up straight away. Promotion above the rank of Staff Nurse, for a man, is rare indeed. Apart from that, everything is just fine. Talk about equal rights for women! The only way they could obtain equal rights in *nursing* is if they *gave up* a few!"

This remark caused laughter from the small group, and I felt comforted. We were all in the same boat, I decided, and this would bond us together.

I found out later that Ron had, in fact, been nursing for some years but had never been offered promotion. As far as I was ever aware, this disappointment never caused bitterness, and he kept a sense of humour. He seemed to fulfil the role of father figure to the group of male nurses and had the reputation for giving advice that was sound.

That first night, he said to me, "Remember that you are in the minority, so all eyes will be on you."

"Rather like being a monk in a nunnery?"

"Exactly right. My best advice to you, if you really want to become a State Registered Nurse, is to look after your patients. Some of them might say they prefer a woman to look after them. That may be so, but the only distinction a really sick patient makes is between good and bad nursing. Sisters and doctors, they can insult you from Land's End to John O'Groats, but if you look after your patient, there's little anyone can do to you."

I was to remember these words in the difficult times ahead.

"Hey, man, don't let him get you too serious!" Tony brandished a bottle of gin. "A toast to our new friend and colleague!"

From tooth-mugs, we drank our mutual health.

CHAPTER TWO
A Thorn Amongst the Roses

The School of Nursing had been built as a large Victorian town house. Surrounded by trees and lawns, it looked attractive in the early morning sunshine.

The first item on the timetable of the first day of training was an instruction to don uniform. Consequently, I was now dressed in white; the loose-fitting smock buttoned to the throat. Which did I resemble more: the dashing American intern as seen on the films, or the unbalanced scientist of a Hammer horror film?

The classroom, with its floor shining like glass, smelled strongly of wax polish. A large blackboard, roll-up screen and a tall desk were sited, predictably, at the far end of the room. To the right of the desk, less predictably, suspended from a metal frame, swung a human skeleton.

As the room filled with students, I looked anxiously round for a fellow male. Finding not a single one, my gaze returned to the skeleton. He was male. And I could swear I detected a look of sympathy from those empty sockets.

"Good morning, everybody. My name is Miss Grayson, your Sister Tutor. Please find a desk and be seated."

A tiny, rotund woman, her grey hair in a neat bun under a quaint cap tied beneath the chin with a large, white bow, addressed us.

I quickly slid into an end desk near a window, not wanting to be hemmed in on all sides.

As she spoke, the Sister Tutor punctuated her speech with a snort, which I decided was caused by trouble with her adenoids.

"May I welcome you to the Victoria Royal Infirmary and to your three months preliminary training course: the first part of the three years it takes to qualify as a State Registered Nurse.

"So that you don't look back and say you came into this work with your eyes closed, I will tell you now that the life of a nurse is far from easy. Some aspects you will find harrowing. You will meet death and suffering at close quarters. You will have to adjust, in order to cope with this.

"Many things will repulse you: the foul-smelling dressings of a fungus-infected cancer, for example; cleaning up a doubly incontinent patient; wiping sputum from the face of a chronic bronchitic. You may have to tend the injuries of a drunken driver who has just knocked down and killed someone, or deal with the parents who have badly mistreated their young baby.

"You will learn to maintain your professional dignity and not to get involved emotionally. This is often very difficult. Long working hours, hard discipline, constant study, and much responsibility will be asked of each and every one of you."

The Tutor looked around at the rows of faces. "Some of you may find you are unable to face up to the rigours of the life and will leave within the first twelve months. Probably half the number here today will be present to sit the final examinations. I can see some of you find this hard to believe, but, sadly, this will be so."

The tiny, elderly Tutor smiled her pleasant smile. "Before you get too downhearted, I would add that nursing brings immense satisfaction. Most of you will find the work both stimulating and interesting and will want to choose no other profession. It will become truly part of your life."

There was a buzz of comment among the student nurses. The girl sitting next to me smiled. "I think I'll resign now; how about you?" she whispered.

"Beat you to the office," I replied, but I laughed.

The Tutor was addressing us once more.

"Your first year will be devoted to the study of Anatomy and Physiology, Hygiene, and Basic Nursing Care. You will be required to pass the General Nursing Council examinations in those subjects before entering your second year of training. Textbook lists will be given out - the books are to be purchased as soon as possible.

"Surgery, Medicine, Pharmacology, Gynaecology, and Psychology will be covered during the second and third years of training. Any questions?"

A young woman with a shock of thick, red hair stood up. All eyes swivelled to see who would be confident enough to put questions at such an early stage.

"Speak up, nurse."

"When are we likely to be dealing with real, live patients?"

"Well, nurse, I sincerely hope that all the patients you come across will be real and certainly alive." The students laughed. "However, before we foist you onto an unsuspecting public, I think we must first satisfy ourselves as to your competence. Sit down, nurse, please."

Next came some dreary regulations: all nurses to be in residence before 10.30 p.m.; no make-up or jewellery allowed when on duty; no members of the opposite sex allowed in the nurses' home at any time; any sickness to be reported to the Home Sister; all beds to be made before going on duty.

I heard one nurse exclaim in a whisper, "I thought we'd come to be nurses, not to join a ruddy convent."

Gathering up her papers, the Tutor announced a coffee break.

Noticing me standing alone, some girls took pity and beckoned me over to join them.

"At least he won't have to bother about make-up or jewellery!" commented one.

"We hope not!" another rejoined. This caused a laugh.

"Don't worry, love, we're all for you," said someone referred to as Sonya. "We were just saying you ought to be awarded the Military Cross for this ordeal. I wouldn't like it, would you, Sue?"

"Oh, I don't know. He's probably thoroughly enjoying himself - aren't you?"

"Well," I said, grinning, "it's beginning to grow on me. I'll get used to it in time."

"Anyway, you've got a full three years," remarked Sonya, encouragingly. She stifled a sleepy yawn.

After the break there followed a period of yet more form-filling and the collection of study papers. With the warning that lateness would not be tolerated at any time, the Tutor dismissed us for the lunch break.

Lunch proved a formidable affair. It was taken in the hospital dining room and we were treated to waitress service. A stern-looking woman in plum-coloured uniform directed us to our places.

"She's the Home Sister, and a real tartar," someone whispered. "If you're even a minute late for your sitting, she sends you out."

When all were seated, the 'tartar' walked to a small table in the corner of the room, and tapped a side plate sharply with a spoon.

Immediately, most of the diners rose to their feet, with others, like me, following anxiously.

"For what we're about to receive, may the Lord make us truly thankful."

"Amen!"

"Blimey, we are in a ruddy convent," whispered the nurse who had made a similar observation earlier that morning.

As we ate, I noted that nurses were placed on tables according to rank or year. Staff Nurses, in purple, sat aloof, or so it seemed to me. The Sisters, who were God I was told, ate in a dining room of their own.

Conversation never grew rowdy. No one challenged the air of strict discipline – with all plates having to be cleared away before the final grace - I felt sympathy for any slow eater, with fifty pairs of eyes watching every mouthful.

"For what we have received, may the Lord make us truly thankful."

"Amen!"

And, duly, in order of rank, we filed out. I realised that the lengthy ritual of the meal had taken up almost all the hour allotted; there was no break from the timetable of the day.

Miss Grayson, the Sister Tutor, introduced a Miss Crawley. "She will take you for the rest of this period, and for most of your Anatomy and Physiology lectures."

Miss Crawley turned out to be a woman devoid of any trace of humour. Moreover, a reputation for tale-telling had made her highly unpopular. She had, not surprisingly, gained the nickname of 'Creepy-Crawley', and many of us, later on in our training, found to our cost that she had been aptly named.

However, she was a good lecturer and soon had us all absorbed in the study of the skeleton.

Bones were passed from hand to hand, as names, types and functions were announced and explained. I enjoyed the very sound of the words: humerus, radius and ulna - the bones of the arm - and femur, tibia and fibula - those of the leg.

We examined the ball-and-socket joints and learned about the special fluid, rather like oil, which lubricates the covering of the bone, thus enabling certain joints to move smoothly next to one another. We were told that we would have to know every bone in detail, and that we would be examined on the knowledge at the end of each week. The whole class groaned.

But the idea uppermost in my mind was the realisation that the construction of the human body was a wonderful thing.

The formidable Miss Crawley was replaced by Miss Grayson once more. Now we were to be instructed in the art of bed-making.

Some of the other students and I found it hard to tear ourselves away from poring over the skeleton - whom we now knew as 'Albert' - so fascinated had we become with the identification of bones.

However, we were admitted to a section of the classroom which had been hidden; this was set out like a hospital ward in miniature - complete with bed, trolleys, screens, medicine cupboards, and all the other paraphernalia that were part of a typical hospital sickroom.

In the bed sat a dummy, staring glassily at the wall opposite.

"You've all met Albert, now let me introduce you to George! He is to be your first real patient."

As the Tutor was speaking, she looked around for a couple of students to act as guinea pigs for her experiment.

"Nurse Wilson and Nurse Butler, come to the front. Let them through, please. Now, I want you to unmake this bed, then make it up again, please. Well? Do get started, nurses! We haven't got all day."

The student nurses stopped staring dumbly at 'the patient', and sprang into action, grabbing the counterpane and pulling it off the patient towards the bottom of the bed, where it was draped over the bed foot. In like manner, the top sheet and blankets were removed, until George was quite uncovered, except for his red-and-white-striped pyjamas. The precarious pile of bedding began to slide and landed in an undignified heap on the floor.

In silence, the Tutor watched.

"Now change the bottom sheet, nurses."

To the horror and entertainment of the audience, the removal of the bottom sheet and the insertion of a clean one appeared to necessitate turfing the patient onto the ward floor.

Amid screams of laughter, the two students struggled on until George was once more under sheet, blankets and counterpane.

"Now, did anyone see anything wrong in that little exercise?"

By raising a hand, Miss Grayson stilled the babble.

"You, nurse. Yes, you." She was looking at me. "Come here. We will now strip this bed, change the undersheet and make it up *properly*."

Chairs were placed end to end at the foot of the bed, to take the neatly folded and piled discarded bedding. George was left with a sheet and a blanket, while the Sister Tutor demonstrated how to roll and hold the patient while changing the bottom sheet.

While she worked, Miss Grayson talked to George as if he were a real human being, asking him how he felt, whether he was cold, did he require anything?

"Never treat the patient like a dummy - and never talk over him," she instructed. "Keep your chat about boyfriends and what you did last night away from the patient. He's not really interested. He wants your attention on him. And you must give this fully at all times."

Under the Tutor's direction, I began to see what an art good nursing was; the whole procedure was made to look so easy. This came, obviously, from practice and from confidence. These were two things I lacked, so far. *Look after your patient*, I thought. Sound advice indeed.

CHAPTER THREE
My First Injection

Over the next few weeks we attempted to learn, by way of lectures and practical instruction, how to care for the sick.

An example of our naivety at this time was our ignorance of the fact that prolonged bed-rest, the old cure-all, itself threw up problems, potentially fatal, for our patients. Now, we learned about pressure sores and those parts of the body most likely to suffer from them. As with anything resistant to treatment, prevention was given great emphasis. From being happily unaware of such nursing conundrums, nightmares indeed, we were now 'in the know', saw such matters as quite obvious, and soon would have the responsibility of dealing with them.

"Today," said Miss Grayson, fixing the student body with the now-familiar glint in her eye, "you are going to learn how to give an injection."

We gazed at the small tray she had brought in with her.

"It is absolutely essential that you all familiarise yourselves with this procedure, as you will be called upon to give injections countless times in your careers."

A syringe was held up for all to see, and we stared, transfixed.

"First, always swab the injection site with spirit. Most of your injections will be given into the buttock, which has plenty of tissue. This is a relatively safe area, but there are dangers. You might hit the sciatic nerve. To avoid this, you make an imaginary cross on the buttock, and then aim for the upper, outer quadrant of the cross, and you should be quite safe. Once the needle is inserted, always withdraw

29

the piston, noting any blood entering the syringe. If you see blood, you must withdraw your syringe, as you may have entered a blood vessel."

As we visualised such dire possibilities, most of us were filled with dread. To get used to the feel of the needle, we were given oranges on which to practise. First came the simple insertion of the needle, and then we graduated to injecting the fruit with sterile water.

"No complaints from your patients, I trust," remarked our Tutor, smiling at our attempts to deal accurately and confidently with the oranges. "Let's hope you get similar responses when attempting the real thing."

My first patient, a chronic bronchitic, looked up at me with a jaundiced eye. "'Ere, you done this before?" He grasped the sheets tightly to his chin.

"Oh, many times!"

"Then, why are you doing it and not her?" He nodded in the direction of the Staff Nurse who was clearly hovering apprehensively in a gap in the screens.

I had no answer to this.

Staff Nurse moved into action. Remonstrating with the patient, she removed his sheet and pyjama trousers, then turned him onto his side, indicating to me that all was ready.

My mouth was dry. I held in my untrained hands what had suddenly grown into an enormous syringe. Now or never. First, *swab*; now the imaginary cross; now *plunge* needle into buttock. This buttock seemed to be all bone, not in the least like a fat, firm orange.

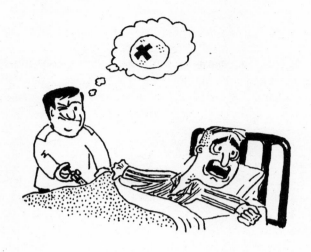

"Bloody hell!" shouted the patient, as I withdrew the needle. "Yon's in the wrong job! He ought to go in for javelin throwing!"

As he rubbed the injection site with a gnarled hand, he glared up at me.

With a sickly grin, I withdrew behind the screens. As I cleared away the injection tray, I tried to convince myself I'd not done too badly. You were *supposed* to be firm and forceful, weren't you? The patient was clearly neurotic; he probably swore at anyone who gave him an injection. Staff Nurse was not reassuring about my clinical competence, however, and I returned to the comparative safety of the classroom, feeling even smaller than when I had ventured out of it a little earlier.

It turned out that few had fared better than I. As fellow students described their experiences, it came to me that I had completely forgotten to check for blood. So, now I was eaten with doubt. Had I, in fact, injected into the wrong area of the buttock? Was it the outer or inner quadrant I had entered?

How I prayed that the patient would not develop a paralysis or an air embolism because of my ineptitude. As no such message came to me from the ward during the following days, I began to relax. I concluded, thankfully, that the patient must have made a straightforward recovery from my nursing skills.

******

After a short break, to celebrate Christmas, granted to us because we were still students, not yet nurses, we moved towards the final tests of the first stage of training.

Although the inevitable personality clashes had occurred, on the whole we had become a close-knit group. No doubt, we were bonded by the herding instincts of the insecure.

As my very last weekly test papers were gathered from my desk, I stared through the classroom window; wisps of snow were falling and I watched a small grey squirrel dart across the lawn. As effortlessly as quicksilver, he streaked up a birch tree and vanished. I felt that I half-envied that squirrel. Not for him the challenges and rigours of hospital life; he would sleep the winter away in some cosy nest, oblivious of me or of the unusual career upon which I had chosen to embark, a career which, I felt, was fraught with difficulty. The difficulties were compounded a hundred fold, it seemed to me, by prejudice against male nurses.

This prejudice, which might become actual hostility in the future, was based upon what? I sat there in the classroom, having completed my final test, and tried to rationalise the anti-male prejudice, as a way of preparing myself to cope with it.

I could fully appreciate, I decided, a male doctor's

preference for having a pretty female to accompany him on his rounds, rather than a gawky male like me. But what about the Sisters? What could their objections be?

I supposed some might resent the intrusion of the male into what had, hitherto, been a totally female profession, just because this was a change, a break with tradition. But, was that, in fact, historically accurate? Hadn't the first nurses been male? For years, monks had cared for the poor and the sick, indeed, long before St Vincent de Paul's Sisters of Charity came onto the scene. Of course, the title 'Sister' was actually a remnant of those times, although I guessed that not all female nurses were aware of that.

Reference to history, though, was not enough in itself to combat prejudice. I must simply have the faith to strive to be a good nurse, a happy nurse, and hope there would prove to be but a few who were actually hostile or obstructive.

******

"As you know, our three-months period of training is now coming to an end." My attention focused once again on Miss Grayson. "You will all be returning here for further tuition in four months' time. The next course will last six weeks. This is called 'block'. You will be in block twice a year, right up to the time you sit your State Final Examination."

What gripped us now was wondering which ward we would be allocated to; it was to be our first real ward experience.

"I have just acquired a copy of the Change List, hot from the press, so to speak. I'll read it out."

Speedily, we each prepared to note down our individual allocations.

"I would point out that the Change List is posted on

33

the hospital notice-board in the main corridor every two months. It is from this list and this list only..." she paused for emphasis, "...that you will discover where your next placement will be. Please do NOT enquire at the School of Nursing, or at Matron's Office, as to where you will be placed next. This information simply will not be given, except in exceptional circumstances." The Tutor paused again, her eyes solemn. "If you are unhappy on a particular ward, then come and discuss the matter with us. We will try to help, but I want to stress that it is better to stay where you are and face up to the problem rather than request a change of ward. Requesting a change of ward is seen as merely running away from one problem towards another."

Miss Grayson read out the allocations and, with my pen poised, I waited.

"Nurse Bolger – Lister Ward - Nurse Simpson – Fleming Ward – her voice droned on."

I guessed Fleming Ward was named after Alexander Fleming the man who discovered penicillin – Lister I knew was another pioneer of medicine who first introduced a form of aseptic technique into hospitals. It would appear that the wards were named after pioneers of medicine, I mused.

Lister Ward, I quickly gathered, was a male surgical unit, run by a Sister Beardmore, a woman with a reputation for fierceness.

"One word of advice." Miss Grayson collected the papers on her desk. "Don't listen to rumours about this and that Sister. Find out for yourselves before coming to a judgement. Some nurses," she gazed round, "I regret to say, delight in putting the fear of God into inexperienced colleagues. You have all now had a good enough basic training to enable you to cope. Don't let silly rumours spoil your first placement. Enjoy it!"

So directing, Miss Grayson swept from the classroom, no doubt, heading straight for Matron's office before the

Change List should be missed.

Amid the agitated throng, I felt a tug at my sleeve.

"We're having an end-of-school drink," said a pleasant, plump-faced nurse called Mary Platts. "You're welcome to join us."

"Where?" Though pleased, I was taken aback by the invitation.

"Do you know "The George," in the centre of town? About nine o'clock."

"I'll be there," I shouted above the din.

******

Later, wallowing in a hot bath, I pondered the future. From comments made by the lads at Wellgate Mount, I gathered that Lister Ward was likely to be no easy placement. Sister Beardmore, I was reliably informed, was not only a 'tartar', but also took an anti-male attitude in her dealings with staff. She delighted, it appeared, in embarrassing male nurses.

Reflecting that the Sister had been nicknamed 'Acid Drop'; I found it hard to take the Tutor's advice to ignore all such talk.

But time and the hot water were both flowing fast, and I leapt from the bath, looking like a boiled lobster. Outside, I turned up my collar and hunched my shoulders against the north wind. A thick coating of snow lay on the pavements, and looking at the footprints of the townsfolk which I tracked and criss-crossed, I wondered idly who had made them. Were they future patients, perhaps?

It was good to cross the threshold of the brightly-lit George, and even more warming to hear a welcoming cheer from the group of student nurses seated at the far corner of the lounge bar.

With my pint of good Yorkshire bitter, I joined the

girls and looked about me. Recently refurbished by the brewery, The George offered plush carpeting, comfortable seating and soft lights. I took a sip of the precious liquid. This was the life!

The girls, now in clothes of their own choice, were in high spirits. As usual, I stood plenty of leg-pulling, being the only male, but I fancy I gave as good as I got.

"I suppose you realise that we all have to be escorted safely home?" Pat Roebuck, an attractive girl, teased.

"Individually, of course!" I replied.

"But, of course!" Pat fluttered her eyelashes like a stage vamp. "Mind you, if each one takes you twenty minutes, you'll get home in about five hours."

Laughter from the group.

"I'd better start now, then. If I'm lucky, I'll get to bed by two a.m. Perhaps the Home Sister'll tuck me in!"

Using the kitty method to pay for drinks, when it was my turn, I ordered sixteen drinks at the bar. Inevitably, the barman passed a remark.

"Excuse me, mate, but how the hell do you do it? Taking two birds out for the night must be great, but fifteen! That's one for the Guinness Book of Records!"

Flattered, and fortified by good company and the best bitter, I whispered conspiratorially, "Actually, I've been commissioned by a wealthy sheikh; this lot are for shipment to Saudi tonight."

The barman's jaw dropped. He'd evidently been helping himself all night. As I heaved up the tray of drinks, I changed tack. "Actually, it's the aftershave that does it. I recommend it, pal - it's called 'Irresistible'."

Coming to see if I needed any help with carrying the drinks, Pat Roebuck chipped in, "It's 'Moth to the Flame', more likely!"

CHAPTER FOUR
Disasters Strike

The sound persisted in its urgency and my hand groped clumsily towards the source of the din. More by luck than by judgement, my fingers found the alarm button and peace was restored. My sleep had been deepened by the alcohol I'd consumed the night before.

This was to be my first day on the ward! My first contact with professionals and patients! Making for the bathroom, I felt the pressure of a dull headache. Teeth-brushing revealed a coated tongue. Back in the bedroom, I admitted to myself that I felt nauseous. I had evidently overdone the convivial drinking and was now feeling very rough and much inclined to crawl back under the blankets.

To go back to bed was, clearly, impossible. Breakfast was out of the question. It was best to make straight for the ward.

On went my uniform: simple, white, 'dental-type' jacket and trousers, with the solitary blue chevrons on the upper arms and the lighter blue epaulettes on the shoulders which denoted my lowly rank as first-year student nurse.

With these insignias on show, surely no one would expect too much of me? With this comforting thought, I left the security of Wellgate Mount and moved, as energetically as possible, towards the hospital and the real beginning of my nursing career.

Feeling uncomfortably conspicuous, I blurted out my name to the Staff Nurse seated behind the desk in the Sister's office.

"Sit down," she said. "We're just about to take report."

As no chair was free, I stood against the wall. A flustered-looking girl, seated nearest to the desk, coughed and squirmed nervously, then began to relate the events of the night shift.

"Mr Fleming, partial gastrectomy, had a fairly comfortable night. His nasogastric tube aspirated hourly and sixty milligrams of water given. Mr Groves, appendicitis, still complaining of slight abdominal pain; nil given by mouth." Now the night nurse gathered fluency. "Mr Lawson, admitted via Casualty with acute retention of urine, catheterised by Dr Whincup; one thousand ml of urine passed, drainage satisfactory. Mr Longdon, carcinoma of stomach, diamorphine, thirty mg, given four-hourly."

"Did this control the pain?" interrupted Staff Nurse.

"Yes, I believe so," the nurse responded.

"Well, did it or didn't it, nurse?"

A long pause.

"The patient slept for most of the night and said he felt comfortable."

"That's better."

The report droned on, until one totally exhausted night nurse, grateful for the relief, left the office for the sanctuary of her bed.

My mind felt badly overloaded. How on earth would I ever be able to give a detailed report like that? Now that the day shift nurses had left to go on to the ward, I was left alone with Staff Nurse.

"I'm Staff Nurse Lomas. You, I take it, are Mr Bolger?"

I nodded. In her late thirties, immaculately turned out, Staff Nurse Lomas wore what seemed to me a slightly severe expression on her otherwise attractive face.

"I haven't the time right now to show you the ward routine," she said, "so I'll get one of the nurses to show you the ropes." She eyed me. "I only hope you're quick on the uptake."

"Quick on the uptake?" I repeated foolishly, thereby seriously prejudicing my chances of impressing her with my lightning intellect.

"Yes," she said, perhaps giving me the benefit of the doubt. "Sister doesn't suffer fools gladly and neither do I." Speedily, she put her head outside the office door. "Nurse!"

Almost at once, a nurse presented herself, and I was introduced to a tall, pleasant-mannered nurse with short, neatly cropped hair.

"Nurse Johnson, show Mr Bolger the routine, will you?"

And Staff Nurse was gone.

Lister Ward struck me as the 'Nightingale' type. Made up of fifteen beds on either side of the long room, plus two single-bed side wards, it was easy to observe the majority of the patients at a single glance, without moving. A table and chair were positioned near the entrance. Halfway down the ward, on the left, was the sluice, or utensil washroom. In the centre of the room stood a highly polished, low cupboard on which several vases of flowers were displayed. Between the outer and inner entrance doors, together with the Sister's office, were the two side wards and a door labelled 'Treatment Room'.

After what seemed to me a hasty whistle-stop tour of the ward, Nurse Johnson led me into the sluice.

"Sister will be 'on' at any time now," she said, "so we haven't much time. Put some disinfectant into a bowl, and grab a cloth and follow me."

Flying out of the sluice and into the ward, with me in her wake, she muttered urgently, "Damp dust."

"Damp dust?"

A look of exasperation came into her eyes. "Yes, dust the windowsills and bed-ends."

I took the opposite side of the room and followed her example, working my way down the ward. Before I'd finished, a loud "Psssst!" interrupted me. "Leave that now. It's time to straighten the beds."

Snatching the bowl and cloth from my hands, she whirled with them into the sluice.

"Now, you must make sure the open end of the pillows faces away from the ward doors," came the instruction. "Sister goes mad if she spots one facing the wrong way!"

Nurse Johnson flashed me a look. "Oh, don't be so glum! You'll get the hang of it. Oh, and the bed wheels - they have to be facing the right way too."

And she kicked the two wheels at the foot of the bed into perfect alignment.

As I straightened the beds, trying to remember the 'right way' to perform each movement, I noticed one particularly ill-looking man, who appeared to have tubes entering every orifice. From the foot of his bed a mass of charts hung. The patient himself lay oblivious to everything. His neighbour, in contrast, was keen to chat.

"'Ow do, lad? Does tha think tha'll like it on 'ere, then?"

"I hope so."

"Tha's not met Dragon yet then, I take it?"

Winking at Nurse Johnson, the man bellowed with merriment.

"Mr Rennard, do be quiet, please," the nurse begged. "She's likely to be on at any minute!"

"Oh, sod 'er, I say. She don't frighten me."

Soon I was aware of a concentrated increase in tempo in the activity around me. All nurses were working as if to an impossible deadline. As though inevitable, the two nurses across the ward collided and a bowl spun into the air, then fell to the floor with a horrible clatter.

At the top of the ward stood Sister Beardmore.

A tall, thickset woman in her early fifties, she wore her black hair short, her eyes a piercing blue. In the dark blue, speckled uniform of a Senior Sister, her most striking feature was her nose; long and sharp, it gave her a heron-like, fish-spearing appearance.

As though recognising who was the 'master', the ward silenced itself until you could have heard the proverbial pin drop, should one have had the temerity to do so. When the last cough had been perpetrated, the last rustle terminated, then, and only then, did Sister Beardmore start her round.

Pausing briefly at the foot of each bed, Sister bade good morning to each patient in turn. Occasionally, she would lift up a chart and inspect it closely, before replacing it. When she came to the sluice, she disappeared from my fascinated view, then reappeared to continue her round.

As she drew near me, I frantically straightened a counterpane. Our eyes met. Hers were entirely, unrelentingly cold. On she went.

"Staff Nurse!" Now, Sister Beardmore stood at her full height, at the top of the ward, hands on hips.

And, of course, the Staff Nurse was instantly in front of her, all anxious attention.

"Who was in charge of this ward last night?"

"That would be Nurse Brooks."

"Then get Nurse Brooks out of bed and back here immediately!"

Sister Beardmore turned on her heels and slammed out of the ward.

Nurse Johnson and I were sent to take a coffee break.

"My God, Sister's in a foul mood this morning!"

"You mean, she isn't usually?" I asked, but without much hope.

At least the effect of the coffee and toast was cheering.

"*Always*. But this morning, possibly fouler than usual!"

"I see. Who are the other two students?"

"The nurse with glasses is Susan Moore, a first-year like you. Janet Russon is a second-year. As you will have gathered," Nurse Johnson raised her eyes towards the three blue lines on her cap, "I'm a third-year." Looking at her watch, she leapt to her feet. "Hell! Look at the time! We were due back three minutes ago!"

As we made with some speed for Co-op Ward, a dejected figure came towards us.

"That's Nurse Brooks. Poor sod's been hauled out of bed to clean up the sluice. Actually, I think Sister's got it in for her."

With eyes to the ground and keeping close to the wall, the night nurse took on the aspect of a pariah, a leper, an outcast. Then she was gone.

"A word of warning," said my companion as we entered the ward. "Keep out of Sister's way and keep busy. Don't forget, we're all in the same boat."

A list of duties lay on the desk. Under the heading 'Male Nurse' was written 'Pubic Shaves' and three names.

"You'll find what you need in the left-hand cupboard in the sluice." Nurse Johnson sped off to carry out her assignments.

I found a tray containing a cut-throat razor, shaving soap and a brush. I filled a gallipot with hot water and placed it on the tray. With all I hoped I needed in the way of accoutrements, I entered the ward.

"Mr Taylor?"

"Aye, lad, that's me," agreed a plump, ruddy-faced man in green-striped pyjamas.

"I've come to give you a shave." I placed the tray on his locker and pulled the screens round.

"I 'ope tha knows what tha's doin' wi' that thing." Mr Taylor stared at the open razor on the tray. "I don't want to end up singing soprano in t' church choir, tha knows."

In fact, I had never used a cut-throat razor in my life.

Having soaped the patient's pubic area well, I picked up the razor. As I manoeuvred around the delicate parts, my hand shook a little.

"Steady, lad, steady." Mr Taylor kept a concerned eye on the proceedings throughout.

I negotiated around a small swelling just above the left groin.

"It's a hernia, lad. Too much liftin' in t' foundry. Been waiting for over a year for treatment."

My next victim was in hospital for a laparotomy, that is, an exploratory operation, and contrasted with Mr Taylor in his emaciation.

"I've not been well for a long time, son. Can't keep anything down," he confided in a weak voice.

"Never mind, you'll soon be up and on the mend."

As I was performing my third and last shave, on a

patient due for an appendectomy, I heard Sister Beardmore's strident voice ringing out orders.

When I could delay no longer, bolstered by the patient's thumbs up gesture, I pulled back the protective screens, took my tray, and returned to the sluice, hoping I wasn't walking towards danger.

The dinner trolley had appeared, when I emerged. Fascinated, I watched Sister Beardmore go through a formal routine of inspecting utensils, then placing them into the steaming food containers. Staff Nurse stood erect as a soldier on parade, gravy ladle in hand. I joined the other nurses, to stand in a queue, tray at the ready. The air was as charged with tension as in an operating theatre.

Glancing at the diet sheet, Sister served the food with amazing speed, and dispatched her nurses to the four corners of the ward.

Having deposited a plate of steamed cod on the bed table of a gastric ulcer patient, I was beckoned over by a well-built man.

"'Ere, mate, any more spuds? Only, this lot wouldn't keep a bloody centipede alive. Ask 'er if I can 'ave some more, will yer?"

Obligingly, I took his plate, noting his bed number, and returned to the trolley.

"What's this?" demanded Sister.

"The patient in bed fifteen would like some more potatoes, Sister."

"More potatoes! *More potatoes!* Bed fifteen! *Bed fifteen!*"

Her face became engorged with blood, her eyes bulged in their sockets. I couldn't help but be reminded of the famous scene in Charles Dickens's Oliver Twist. Could Sister be a descendant of Mr Bumble, the mean and corrupt beadle?

"I don't answer to bed numbers! Go and get the name

of the patient!"

Breathless, I was back. "Mr Glaves, Sister."

Sister Beardmore reared up to her full height and, with hand on hips, as was so typical, she shouted down the ward:

"MR GLAVES! You are, as well you know, on a reducing diet! Do NOT attempt to pull the wool over my eyes by conning my nurses, no matter how stupid they may be. I had intended to allow you a little egg custard for dessert; that is now OFF!"

Subdued silence from bed fifteen.

Speaking slowly, as if to an imbecile, Sister Beardmore addressed me.

"That you are new to this ward has not escaped me. That you are stupid I am just beginning to realise. Take this plate back to Mr Glaves. And do not, in future, quote bed numbers at me."

As I hurried away, I heard her speak to the Staff Nurse. "Get that male person to clean out the lockers; that should suit his level of intellect!"

"Don't let her get you down," whispered Nurse Johnson. "We all cop it, from time to time, so keep your chin up."

******

Wedged between the bedpan washer and the specimen cupboard, I reflected on things: my first day on the ward and already I was in Sister's bad books; she would almost certainly 'have it in for me' in future, and there were eight weeks to go! What total disaster. How was I going to cope? I could resign. Yes, that was it. I'd simply resign.

"Ah! There you are. You're to go to lunch." Staff Nurse Lomas had laughter in her eyes. "You're to clean lockers when you come back. That should keep you out of mischief for a bit!" As I nodded, she gave me a broad wink.

"My God, what a morning," I complained to Nurse Russon, as we made for the dining room.

"Could be worse! It seems Staff Nurse likes you, so you've a friend at court, so to speak. Now, when they *both* have it in for you, it's ruddy murder!"

I noticed that Nurse Russon had a cast in one eye, but what impressed me most was her attractive personality. Her attempt to encourage me was working; I would not resign just yet - at least, not until I'd eaten my lunch.

******

The job of getting down on my knees and cleaning out lockers had two distinct advantages, I reckoned. For one thing, it kept me away from the apparently merciless attentions of Sister Beardmore; more importantly, perhaps, the work enabled me to get to know the patients better.

"Take an apple, lad. Go on, take it!" exhorted Mr Prendergast, as I sorted out his fruit supply lodged at the bottom of his locker. "Wife must think I'm a blinking monkey, she brings such quantities of the stuff." He mimicked an ape, by scratching under his armpits; it came as a relief to have a laugh.

"What are you in for?" I took a surreptitious bite out of a smooth, green Granny Smith.

"Let me put it this way to you, lad: I've got piles of trouble! Ha! Haemorrhoids, to be exact, and bloody painful they are, too, I can tell you! Though which is more terrible, bearing the pain or going in for the knife, I don't know."

"At least they'll get to the bottom of the trouble," suggested the patient in a neighbouring bed.

"Oh, very comical," Mr Prendergast responded. "I hope they go light on the anaesthetic when they strip your veins!"

Some patients, of course, were too ill to chat or crack

jokes. As I knelt beside them, I could only guess at the nature of their problems.

Suddenly, the word came. We could go. I had actually survived a full shift!

All clearing up tasks in the sluice I did with supreme care. There was always tomorrow of which to beware. The relief nurses looked at me with curiosity, as I joined my colleagues outside Sister's office.

Nurse Johnson coughed nervously, smoothed down her apron and knocked at Sister's door.

"Come!"

The nurse looked in. "May we go off duty, Sister?"

"Are all the fluid charts up to date? Have you left the ward tidy?"

"Yes, Sister."

"Very well, you may go. But woe betide you in the morning if I find all is not well."

"Yes, Sister. Thank you, Sister."

As Nurse Johnson bowed out, closed the door carefully, then gave us the victorious thumbs up, a picture of the wretched Nurse Brooks, slinking, humiliated, down the corridor, visited my mind.

But uppermost was the delighted feeling of relief. Away we all walked, slowly at first, then with quickening steps, until we were practically running.

CHAPTER FIVE
Life Has its Up and Downs

My spell of training on Lister Ward taught me an art not to be found in any nursing textbook: the art of appearing busy.

The reason for this was that Sister Beardmore could be counted on to deal a severe blasting to any nurse who seemed to her to be insufficiently active, and I knew that, of all the staff on the ward, I was the least likely to escape her wrath. So a strategy had to be found to cope with such quiet periods as visiting times.

Ron passed on a few 'tricks of the trade', as he put it, in this respect. One which proved useful time and time again was simple, indeed basic: the urinal trick. All that was required to make this work was the co-operation of the patients, and one urinal. This item was hidden at the back of a patient's locker. If pounced on and challenged, I would say, "Just going to empty a urinal, Sister."

"Well, get on with it then!" was the usual tart rejoinder. By the time I had collected the article and borne it away to the sluice, Sister Beardmore would be giving her best attention elsewhere. The minute it was safe to do so, the urinal would be deposited in a different part of the ward, ready for the next panic. Such were the ludicrous lengths one was forced to go to in order simply to survive!

That Sister Beardmore put her patients first, and that they were extremely well and efficiently cared for, I have no doubt at all, and indeed would testify to that. But, equally, it was unquestionable that her regime, her methods of discipline, were over-harsh, and that I, as a man, an *intruder* perhaps, excited her worst hostilities.

I owed so much at this crucial time to the efforts of my fellow staff and of the patients on the ward. Nurses would conspire to keep me out of trouble, and patients, quite marvellously, strove to cheer me up.

In spite of worries, humiliations and setbacks of various kinds, I was starting to enjoy the nursing life enormously. This feeling of satisfaction was heightened by being introduced to the hospital world that lay beyond a programme of pubic shaves, dealing with bedpans and cleaning the sluice.

"Would you like to accompany me on the dressing round?"

The sound of Sunday morning church bells filtered through the ward. It was Sister Beardmore's weekend off, otherwise Staff Nurse Lomas's proposal would have been totally out of the question.

"You can be my dirty nurse," she announced.

Noting the expression on my face, she elaborated, laughing. "I'll be scrubbed up, you see, so your job will be to handle anything not sterile and to pour solutions and the like. You'll see."

So, in mask and gown, I walked alongside Staff Nurse Lomas, pushing the trolley.

"Mr Marsh?"

"Yes, that's me." The patient was a thin, bespectacled, middle-aged man and he spoke in a thin, weak voice.

Staff Nurse gave me the nod to draw the screens round.

"We've come to look at your wound. Mr Marsh," she continued, removing the dressing to reveal a pink, fleshy protrusion from the abdomen, "has a colostomy."

I stared, transfixed.

"Pour me some saline; you'll find it beneath the trolley." Using forceps, the Staff Nurse carefully cleaned around the wound. "Mr Marsh had an obstruction of the lower bowel. It had to be removed. His motions will now come through this opening into a special bag. We will be fixing that on in a short while, but not just yet." Replacing the soiled dressing with a clean one, she gave the man a smile.

The wound of our next patient stretched across his lower abdomen; it looked pink and healthy. I counted fifteen black catgut sutures, stitched at regular intervals.

"Now, with Mr Smedley, we're going to remove alternate sutures."

"Oh?"

"Well, we need to test that the wound is fully healed, then we can remove the rest."

Using forceps and scissors, Staff Nurse deftly severed the selected sutures just above the knot. Keeping a keen eye on the snipping, Mr Smedley sensed an interested audience.

"I've had a prostate removed, nurse," he volunteered, giving me my correct title. "Went out for a few pints one night, and found I couldn't pee. I was in a right state, I can tell you! Well, I'd supped must be six or seven pints, you see!"

Staff Nurse Lomas took up the story. "The prostate is a gland situated at the base of the bladder. In normal health it's about the size of a walnut, but in older men it can enlarge. The urethra, the tube that carries urine from the bladder, passes through the prostate and can actually be squeezed shut. Hence Mr Smedley's predicament. As an emergency measure, a catheter has to be inserted into the bladder to drain off the urine, until surgery can take place." She paused, and smiled at me. "You, as a male nurse, will be expected to learn this technique, as, in this hospital, only male doctors and nurses are allowed to catheterise males." Maybe I pulled a face. Staff Nurse Lomas laughed. "Don't worry. You won't be expected to do this just yet!"

"Thank God for that," exclaimed the patient. "I thought you were going to let him practise on me, and I reckon I've been through quite enough already!"

Clearing away the dressing trolley in the treatment room, I thanked Staff Nurse Lomas for her clandestine tuition.

"We all have to learn," she pointed out, smiling, "so, think nothing of it."

While some of the females in this profession seemed dead against me as a man and therefore as an unusual, not to say alien part of the ward team, others, such as Staff Nurse Lomas, appeared to be all for me, offering encouragement and opportunities to develop.

******

My volume of *Surgery for Nurses* slipped from my hands and fell to the floor as Ron bounced on the end of my bed.

"We call ourselves the Wellgate Five," he announced, "the most sought-after bachelors in the hospital. Why don't you join us? Our next appearance is at the dance on Saturday night. Coming?"

"Do me a favour." David Muller walked into the room, still brushing his teeth. "The last dance we went to was a bloody disaster, and you know it."

"What went wrong?" I wanted to know.

Muller waved his toothbrush in the air.

"I'll tell you what went wrong: we were outnumbered, three to one, by junior doctors and male medical students. We didn't stand a chance!"

"Oh, don't worry, it'll be different this time."

Muller poked Ron in the chest with his toothbrush.

"OK, I'll bet you ten bob you don't pull anything all night."

"Done! You're on. You're a witness, Mike."

"Right. Now clear out, the pair of you. The new lad's got some studying to do."

"Swot! Swot!"

Laughing, they ducked the thrown textbook and left.

Finding my place in the retrieved volume once more, I recognised a degree of excited anticipation at the thought of the following Saturday night's 'hop'.

******

He was called John; a smashing lad, about my age. I had got to know him fairly well in the few weeks I'd been working on Lister Ward. John had been admitted for routine investigations, but the laparotomy revealed a large, malignant mass in the bladder, which had already spread to other organs. Nothing could be done. All that remained, in theatre, was to sew him back together and return him to the ward.

"Mike, I keep talking to people who aren't there. Why is that?"

John was on regular doses of diamorphine. Soon after he made this remark to me, he lapsed into merciful unconsciousness, and during the same afternoon he died.

With his family, I shared the experience of waiting, waiting for the inhalation that never came. I myself felt instantly bereaved; that he was so young, that he should have had most of his life in front of him, shocked me deeply.

Sister Beardmore instructed Nurse Johnson to show me how to perform the 'last offices'.

"Right, you must set up the trolley." Nurse Johnson was quiet in her manner, and sensitive. "On the bottom shelf we need a shroud, a sheet, bandages, cotton wool, forceps, and a needle and cotton. Okay? Oh, and two mortuary labels. You'll find them in Sister's desk, top right-hand drawer."

My trolley set up, I knocked at Sister's office.

"Come."

Sister Beardmore had company, a younger Sister, who looked amused as I presented myself before them.

Sister glared. "What do you want?"

"Two mortuary labels, please, Sister."

"Top right-hand drawer." She turned her back and resumed her conversation.

As I left the office, clutching the labels, I heard the visiting Sister enquire: "How do you find him?"

"Useful for lifting - that's about it," came the caustic reply.

"Yes," her colleague concurred.

"I always think there's something odd about a man who wants to make beds!"

******

Carrying out 'last offices' proved a distressing experience. Working quietly behind the screens, Nurse Johnson explained the procedures in a whisper.

"First, we have to remove the pillows and straighten John out. Rigor mortis will set in shortly."

I noticed she handled John's body as carefully as if he were still alive. She pushed a pillow under the dropped jaw, partially pushing the mouth shut. Then two pieces of dampened cotton wool were placed over each eyelid.

"That's as far as we go for now." She pulled a sheet over the corpse.

"Why's that?" Though distressed, I was puzzled.

"As a sign of respect, and to give the body fluids time to settle down. It is also thought that it is in the first hour the soul leaves the body."

An hour later, we returned. Now the young man's face had taken on a wax-like appearance, with the eyes a little more sunken.

After stripping, the body was washed thoroughly from head to foot, the hair was combed, the orifices were all plugged, and the jaw was tied in place with a bandage.

Now we put the shroud on the body; it resembled an open-backed nightshirt with a frilly collar. The patient's arms and hands were placed down by his sides, with the palms down.

Finally, the damp cotton wool was taken off the eyes, the labels were fixed, and the body was wrapped in the sheet.

Silently, we stood a while, surveying our handiwork. It seemed so strange to me that this mute, sheeted figure had been a living being, my exact contemporary and so good-natured, only a short while earlier.

Did you ever get used to death? Did you, in fact, become blasé about it? I hoped not.

"We have to screen the ward off before the mortuary trolley arrives," Nurse Johnson whispered, and I was brought back to practicalities.

We got busy, but this part of the routine struck me as somewhat absurd, as the patients were well aware of what was happening.

"Gone, has he?" Mr Prendergast, the patient with haemorrhoid trouble, hardly needed confirmation as I drew the screens round his bed. Perhaps saying anything was better than silence, better than pretence. "Poor little sod's better off out of it, if you ask me!"

When all patients had been screened off, the mortuary trolley trundled on to the ward, then swiftly vanished with its tragic cargo.

The ward refused to return to normal, in spite of Sister Beardmore's false joviality.

"What's the matter with you all?" she challenged heartily. "Come along, it's no good just lying there, staring at the ceiling!"

When I left the ward that evening, I felt that I had experienced more of death and dying in that one shift than most people would experience in a lifetime. That, I supposed, was nursing.

******

Clifton Hall, conveniently near the hospital, was a seedy-looking building in desperate need of a coat of paint. In its time it had served as a church, then as a cinema. Now it doubled as a bingo and dance hall.

Having first visited The Grapes, for a spot of Dutch courage, the Wellgate *Six* approached in high spirits.

I found myself leading the way through the predominantly female hubbub to the end of the hall where most of the males were gathered.

A sudden roll of the snare drums. A crash of cymbals. The five-piece band played, but the dance floor remained empty. Now the lights dimmed and a solitary silver globe, suspended from the ceiling, began to rotate, sending a thousand silver stars flickering across the floor and over the assembled faces.

With impressive confidence, a few couples began, rather self-consciously, to rotate in the largely empty space.

I became aware that both Ron and David had already spotted the girl of their dreams. Awkwardly, they had both alighted upon the same third-year nurse. Attired in a close-fitting white blouse and black mini-skirt, she was certainly very striking. But I felt daunted by what I perceived as hardness in her expression. In a throng of females, she stared ahead, her body swaying to the rhythm of the music; she appeared to see nothing, yet take in everything.

"I saw her first," Ron claimed, straightening his tie and smoothing down his well-oiled hair. "Sorry, Dave, but all's fair in love and war." And off he strolled to make his conquest.

In response to his invitation, we could see the nurse studying him in a cool manner. Then her brightly painted mouth turned down in what looked to me like an ugly snarl. She appeared to my fellow, would-be lip-readers to mutter something like "Drop dead!"

Inspired by our mixture of alcohol and nervousness, we doubled up with laughter as Ron, attempting to regain his robbed dignity, kept his head up high and sauntered back.

"Right," said Dave. Although he had been the one, back at base, to doubt the success of the evening, he spoke jauntily enough. "Right, just watch an expert at work."

This time, the young woman's retort seemed to be even more devastating, and Dave had his head down as he retired, beaten.

"Do you know the definition of an 'expert'?" quipped Ron, as Dave rejoined us. "Well, 'ex' is a has-been, and 'spurt' is a drip under pressure."

Laughter.

"Anyway, we're splitting, man," said Jimmy, on behalf of himself, Tony and Raj.

"Don't go. There are plenty more fish in the sea!" Ron exclaimed.

"Look, man, we've seen it all before. They're not interested in male *nurses,* especially not black ones."

"Hey, will you look at that!" Dave murmured.

We watched a young man take the now-smiling object of Ron and Dave's desire onto the dance floor and, instantly, the couple were engaged in a smoochy foxtrot.

"Fifth-year medical student!" Ron was disgusted.

"I told you," pointed out Dave. "Happens every bloody time."

Suddenly, I saw a familiar face: Nurse Johnson from Lister Ward. She was always very easy to get on with; surely she'd not turn me down?

"Watch the new boy," I said, and began the long walk.
But the smile faded from Nurse Johnson's face.

"I'd love to, Mike, I really would, but I'm with my
boyfriend."

She seemed nervous as she explained he was at the 'gents', but would be back any minute. Even to one as young and unsophisticated as myself, her words seemed to intend a 'gypsy's warning', and smiling, I retreated. Out of the corner of my eye, I was aware of a great hulk of a bloke looming into view and was relieved that I'd not outstayed my welcome.

Of course, I took my share of the laughter. But now, apparently, even the hopeful Ron had had enough.

"I vote a quick pint, then fish and chips all round. All those in favour, say 'Aye'."

There followed a resounding "Aye!"

Hands deep in pockets, egos deeply battered, we trudged our way to the nearest pub.

"Didn't fancy any of 'em, anyway," said Ron.

"Nor me," Dave echoed.

Thus, on this sobering Saturday night, three of the Wellgate six found themselves, on this point, in fervent agreement.

CHAPTER SIX
How the Other Half Live

'Casualty', it said against my name on the new change list pinned to the notice board. That was a puzzle: accident and emergency experience was normally reserved for second- or even third-year students.

Back at our digs, Tony, one of the black nurses, explained the apparent deviation from the rules. The reason for this early placement was due to the fact that several staff had succumbed to a particular nasty 'flu bug, hence my early placement.

With the thought that soon I would be free from Sister Beardmore and her tyrannous empire forever, I took up duty on Lister Ward in the lightest of spirits. Perhaps, for that very reason, I suffered an accident that morning: I broke a thermometer. Horrors! I saw Mrs Fitt, a nursing auxiliary of treacherous repute, heading with indecent speed for Sister's office.

"Bloody hell, that's blown it," remarked the patient I was attending. I was inclined to agree.

Soon came the much-dreaded summons.

"So, you've broken a thermometer?" Sister Beardmore glared at me across her desk. "That you've not seen fit to report this matter to me, I regard as a most serious breach of discipline. I am, therefore, sending you to Matron."

I suppose I was open-mouthed. That I had not had time to report the matter seemed to be irrelevant.

"While you're about it," she barked, rummaging in her drawer, "you may as well take these with you." Into my hand was thrust an envelope containing thermometer particles. "Six in all, now." In Sister's eyes there was a nasty gleam of triumph.

Mystified, I joined a queue of miserable-looking nurses leaning against a pale blue wall. As the door to Matron's office closed behind each nurse in turn, the sound of a raised voice could clearly be heard. This contrasted with a period of utter silence just before the nurse, pale, with eyes down, left the office, hesitated, then gratefully left the scene.

I was reminded of caged birds who, on release, leave the cage with exuberance, hover, then vanish, never to be seen again. The queue lengthened behind me. It came as a shock when I realised the poor wretch at the head of the line of miscreants was me.

As I entered the office, I reflected that the last time I had appeared in this office had been in far happier circumstances, on the day of my interview. The outcome on that occasion had been all I had hoped for. Now, I wasn't sure what might be the best I could expect.

Matron appeared as a concentration of fury and spite.

"Well? What do *you* want?"

"I've been told to bring these, Matron."

She took the envelope and, wordlessly, tipped the contents on to the desk. Surveying the glass shards, she looked like a fortune-teller casting the 'runes'.

"How many thermometers are here?"

"Er, six. Six, Matron." My sense of foreboding increased.

Her voice quivered with temper. "How *dare* you come here with this amount of breakages! This amount of damage is absolutely inexcusable and will go on your record! Good God, man, you've not been here more than a few weeks. You must be a complete oaf."

With Matron's lecture clanging in my ears, I returned the envelope of new thermometers to an unremorseful

Sister Beardmore. Entirely innocent of all but one of the breakages, I felt like the messenger of old, who is punished by summary execution for bringing bad tidings.

******

Sister Fairburn darted about the Casualty Department like a whippet. I was to learn later that she operated under the delusion that only she could be trusted to carry out treatments properly. On my first morning, I was relieved by her friendly manner.

"We run a tight ship here. Now, there are six treatment cubicles, as you can see." Each cubicle was furnished with a single couch protected by a white paper strip. "This is the resuscitation area."

I noted the suction and oxygen equipment, which were positioned ready to hand. An operating lamp was suspended above a theatre table. Several trolleys surrounded the table, their contents hidden by green, sterile sheets. To me, the atmosphere was electric. It was as though we were on stage and at any moment a drama would erupt.

"We get almost anything in here," Sister Fairburn elaborated. Leaning against a wall, she observed me. "Road traffic accidents, overdoses, stab wounds, drunks, heart attacks. You name it, we get it."

"How do you cope?" Adrenaline pumped through me at the mere thought of all these challenges, so various in their treatments.

"We cope."

The tour ended in the plaster room, where the orderly was about to start work on a Pott's fracture of the wrist. The patient, a middle-aged woman, informed us she had been running for a bus when she slipped, and had put out her hand to save herself.

Sister lifted up the injured arm carefully. "A Pott's fracture resembles a dinner fork, bent. Now, don't forget, 'dinner fork deformity' is absolutely diagnostic of a Pott's fracture of the wrist."

We left the plaster room as the orderly dipped what looked like a roll of white bandage into a bucket of water and swiftly applied it to the patient's forearm and wrist.

Back at the central treatment area, I was introduced to the rest of the staff, consisting of a junior Sister called Gregg, a Staff Nurse Collier, and two Enrolled Nurses, Dobson and O'Malley. All, with one exception, looked friendly and welcoming. The Staff Nurse, however, gave me a look of bored contempt, and then studied her nails as objects more worthy of her interest.

Dr Monk, a fresh-faced man, not long out of medical school, was the Casualty Officer, and I took to him straight away. He gave me a sly wink.

"Don't be put off by Old Sullen-Drawers here," he said, jerking his thumb towards Staff Nurse Collier. "Definitely a case of bluebeltitis, if ever I saw one."

"Bluebeltitis?"

"Yep. Just got her blue belt and thinks she's God."

The Staff Nurse cast him a look of pure venom, but this had little effect on the doctor.

Apparently oblivious to this banter, Sister explained that there were two other students, who were both on study leave for the next two weeks. "So," she concluded cheerfully, "you're our one and only student, for the time being. We should be able to keep you busy all right! Let's see. Nurse Dobson, would you take Mr Bolger with you this morning?"

Nurse Dobson smiled, and we walked off.

"We'll start on treatments." She explained that, after patients had been seen by the Casualty Officer, any treatment he prescribed was written on a card. The cards were then placed in first-come-first-served order by the Reception Clerk, who eventually placed the cards on a large wooden tray on her desk.

"Right, let's get cracking, shall we?"

At our approach, the patients on the long wooden benches in the waiting area looked up expectantly.

"Mr Bower?" called Nurse Dobson.

"That's me." A middle-aged man in greasy overalls hobbled towards us, clutching his boots to his middle.

"Cubicle One, Mr Bower!"

Nurse Dobson pulled the treatment card from beneath her bib and then handed it to me. The barely legible scrawl read: 'Second degree burns to left foot, apply paraffin tulle dressing.'

"Hot slag what done it." Mr Bower slid onto the couch with difficulty. The burn looked nasty and deep. Nurse Dobson prepared to clean the area before applying the dressing.

Just then, the screens flew back and Sister Fairburn entered the cubicle. Picking up the patient's treatment card, she exclaimed, "I'll see to this; you attend to the patient in resuscitation."

With a look of complete exasperation, Nurse Dobson left, without saying a word.

"Don't just stand there. Go with her! You'll never learn anything by simply standing about."

Nurse Dobson must have seen the puzzled look on my face. "You'll get used to it," she said. "She's not a bad Sister, but completely disorganised. Doesn't know her arse from her elbow at times."

Laughing, we entered 'resuscitation', where we encountered two ambulance men transferring a patient from a trolley onto the treatment table. Rivers of blood streamed from an obvious scalp wound, poured across the patient's face, then gushed down onto a heavily

63

blood-soaked shirt.

"What's the story behind this?"

"We picked him up at the Midland Station, nurse," explained one of the ambulance crew. "Appears to have lacerations to the scalp, but he won't say how he got them. Probably been in a fight and got clobbered with a bottle."

Having thanked the busy ambulance men, Nurse Dobson took a closer look at the patient.

"Now," she said brightly, "what have you been up to?"

Clinging grimly to a large dressing pad which covered his head, the patient failed to respond. Sally, the receptionist, came in with the treatment card. The nurse read it.

"Mr McLoughlan from Glasgow. Come on, Mr McLoughlan, let's have a look at your scalp."

"No!" The patient spoke with a broad Scots accent. "Get the hell away from me, will ye?" Then he added, "I'll talk to hem, and only hem." He was peering up at me.

"Well, be quick about it. We've got other patients to see to besides you."

Nurse Dobson stepped back, and I drew closer to the man.

"I've had a ruddy hair transplant, all right?" he hissed.

"A hair transplant?"

"Yes, a ruddy hair transplant. Came all the way from Glasgow for it. Oh, the embarrassment of it all!"

"Look," I said, impressed by his distress, "let me get the Casualty Officer, at least, and let us try to stop the bleeding."

"OK. But no women, mind. or I'd fade away wi' the shame of it all.

Half an hour later, the patient was discharged, a pressure-pad dressing attached firmly to the top of his head.

"What was it, exactly, that caused all that bleeding?" I

64

asked Dr Monk, as he ripped off his surgical gloves.

"Ah, well, hair transplants, you see, consist of plugs of hair being removed from the back of the neck and transplanted into the scalp. In our unlucky patient's case, he was running for his train, and this caused the plugs to pop up. The scalp bleeds very easily, as you will have noticed, hence the terrific blood loss. Treatment was simple, really: just apply pressure to the plugged area, and allow nature to take its course. A case of hair today, gone tomorrow, really - if you'll forgive the pun!"

******

"Mike, nip up to the Path Lab and take these bloods for cross matching," said Dr Monk,

"Our patient has a suspected perforated gastric ulcer and will need surgery immediately."

I grabbed hold of the two specimen bottles and sped up the steps heading towards the Path Lab with all due haste. At the top of the stairs I paused briefly before walking swiftly on down the main corridor towards my destination. I now became conscious of the lone solitary figure of a Hospital Domestic. I don't know why, but she looked fragile and vulnerable somehow, kneeling there, with scrubbing brush in hand. I watched as she dipped the brush in a bucket then applying a liberal amount of carbolic soap to the bristles, she proceeded to work her arms in repetitive sweeping movements, side to side, side to side. Pausing briefly she straightened her aching back, wiping the back of her rough well-worn hand across her forehead. Bending down once more she removed a cloth from the bucket, wringing this out, she then proceeded to remove the suds deposited by the brush in the same monotonous side-to-side motion.

Suddenly round the far end of the corridor strode none

other than Sir Giles Kendall, Professor of Surgery and Head of the Board of Examiners, a formidable character indeed. Following in his wake I spied no less than 20 white-coated personages made up of Senior Registrars, Housemen and Medical Students. Sir Giles' reputation was legendary and was one of academic brilliance and standards of excellence. In awe, I stood aside to let the entourage pass, pressing myself flat against the wall of the corridor, for I was now level with the cleaner. Unexpectedly, Sir Giles stopped in his tracks, causing his followers to bang into one another like so many shunted railway carriages; they were now in complete disarray. Then, to my amazement, the great man knelt down beside the lone domestic. Placing an arm around her shoulders he spent a few moments in private conversation with her, before standing up and speeding off down the corridor once more, followed by his white coated team. Mystified I moved off towards my destination.

Returning from the Path Lab I spied the cleaner once more still hard at it. On closer look she was old beyond her years, with scraped back hair prematurely greying, yet her face had dignity and a certain pride in it. As I passed her once more I felt compelled to speak, "Not much more to do now, love." I said with a smile.

"No Lad," she replied, "but I don't much care now since the Professor had a word with me."

She must have seen my puzzled look and gave a pleasant laugh. "He operated on my husband some four weeks ago. He was asking how he was and said for me to contact him if I was worried - wasn't that kind, fancy him remembering me!"

I felt suddenly moved by this whole experience and humbled. I had without doubt been in the presence of greatness. Later on that day I recounted the tale to Dr Monk. He looked thoughtful then said, "that sounds characteristic of the big man, that's why he is so respected."

"I remember some years ago a recently qualified colleague of mine arrived at hospital late at night, carrying two heavy suitcases. Sir Giles, who lived in at the time, had a habit of taking late night strolls around the hospital - never a one for grand clothes - he was wearing an old mac. Mistaking him for an off-duty porter my friend asked for directions to the Junior Doctors' Residence."

"Top of the Drive, First Left," said the Prof.

"Would you like to earn yourself a shilling and carry one of my suitcases?" enquired my pal.

With little prompting Sir Giles grabs one of the suitcases and proceeds with him up the drive. Standing outside the front door he duly accepts his tip and disappears into the night. Imagine my pal's dismay when some two days later onto the ward troops Sir Giles Kendall at the head of his retinue.

"Thank God he's not recognised me", he thought, as head down he joined the ward round. However, before leaving the ward Sir Giles paused, then looked straight at him.

"By the way, young man, thank you for the shilling, it bought me a very nice cup of tea, but don't be so quick to judge a book by its cover in future!"

******

The Casualty Department was the shop window of the hospital. I found it a fascinating place to work. Saturday night looked like becoming my favourite shift, the first one produced so many dramas. In Casualty, one came in contact with the flotsam and jetsam of society: drunks, prostitutes, pimps, drug addicts, to name but a few categories. Some of these people were entirely harmless, while others could be quite dangerous if not handled with tact and diplomacy.

Drunks were always tricky to deal with. They came, I found, under one of two headings: silly-daft or plain bloody nasty. One of the first I had to deal with came in the first classification. The man came staggering into Casualty, clutching his crotch through blood-soaked trousers.

"What the devil have you been up to?" But all Sister Fairburn got from him was gibberish. "Get him into a cubicle and onto a couch. I'll fetch Dr Monk."

With some difficulty, I manoeuvred the man onto a couch. "Now," I said, in a business-like manner, "let's get these trousers off, shall we?"

Coinciding with my attempt to pull down the patient's zip came an almighty howl. The words that followed would have made a ship's parrot blush. Through further investigation, I found that the zip was jammed solid.

Dr Monk's head appeared round the screens. "The trousers will have to be cut off. Got any scissors?"

"Yes." I produced a pair from my top pocket.

"Then, let's get cracking, and see what all this is about." The doctor snatched the scissors from my wavering hand. Within seconds, he had cut round the immovable zip.

"Ere! What the bloody 'ell's going on?" The patient half raised himself on his elbows.

"Right, one leg each: ready, steady, pull!"

The trousers came away with a jerk.

"Good God." Dr Monk took a closer look. "How on earth have you managed this?"

We both stared down in amazement at the patient's private parts. Instead of zipping up his flies, he had somehow zipped up his penis. There was no mistaking it: the zip was firmly attached to the member, from base to tip.

"Bring the suture trolley from resuscitation. We'll have to get this thing off."

The whole procedure was more than enough to make your eyes water. I had to fight a strong urge to turn my head away. The fact that the patient was stupefied by drink stood him in good stead. While I held him, Dr Monk administered a local anaesthetic. Each time the needle struck home, the scene was reminiscent of an American rodeo show, I being the rider, the patient the bucking bronco.

Once the zip had been removed with a scalpel, no less than twelve stitches were inserted into the patient's manhood.

While waiting for a taxi, in between gulps of black coffee, the man told me his sorry tale.

"Must have supped at least ten pints, busting for a leak, see, so I went to the gents. Thought I'd put me dick away. Anyway, it was then that the bloody zip jammed. I tugged and tugged at it. Well, you would, wouldn't you? Then suddenly, it unjammed and ran easy again." He looked at me. "Funny thing, I didn't feel a bloody thing at the time, but, by Christ, can I feel it now!"

Wordlessly, he made his way towards the exit, where the cab awaited him. As a male, I watched him with the utmost sympathy as he took each slow step.

******

Towards the end of my fourth week in Casualty, I received a summons to Sister Fairburn's office. Her smile was friendly; it would appear I had committed no crime. I was glad, having settled well in the Department, where I was finding the work, with its panics and variety, exceedingly rewarding. Even the aggressive attitude of Staff Nurse Collier had not affected my buoyancy.

"Bit of bad news, Nurse Bolger, I'm afraid. Do come

and sit down." Taking a seat, I was mystified.

"You're leaving us. It appears they are short on nights."

I stared glumly at the floor. "When do I start?"

"Monday. Report at the Night Sister's office at nineteen-thirty hours prompt. I'm very sorry about this; it's most unusual and irregular. But Matron's ways are not always our ways." She beamed at me. "Perhaps you'll have the chance to join us again later on."

The shuffle of papers on her desk told me the interview was over.

"Damn and blast it," said Dr Monk. "Just when I get a bit of male company, you're off. It's too bad!"

Staff Nurse Collier sniggered. "Perhaps we ought to leave the two of you to kiss goodbye."

"Oh, that's nasty!" Nurse Dobson exclaimed.

"Well, you know as well as I do what they say about male nurses!"

"Honestly, you can be a real bitch at times, Collier."

"Oh, get stuffed, Dobson." And Staff Nurse Collier flounced away.

Although the rest of the team went out of their way to be extra friendly and encouraging to me, for the first time since starting in Casualty, I was glad when the shift ended.

"You look down in the dumps, Mike. What's the trouble?" asked Ron, as he, Dave and I were having a drink at The Grapes that night.

"I know I do," I said, staring into my glass, reflecting that, while I needed a second pint, I could probably not afford it. "I've been given the heave-ho from Casualty. I'm to start nights."

"That's a bit rough, when you were enjoying it so much. And you haven't been there long," remarked Dave.

Inspired by their comradely sympathy, I elaborated on the reasons for my depression.

"To add insult to injury," I downed my beer dregs in one, then slammed the pint glass on the table, "it was inferred by a certain Staff Nurse that I'd got the hots for Dr Monk!"

Dave didn't seem shocked, more amused. "Oh, I didn't think he was your type!"

"That'll be Staff Nurse Collier!" Ron pulled a face. "I'd not pay the slightest attention to anything she has to say."

"Luckily," said Dave, "no one does."

"Now, listen." Ron took a hefty swig, and then wiped his mouth with the back of his hand. "It's time I put you straight on one or two things. I told you when you first started in this game that all eyes would be on you."

I nodded. "I remember. 'Monks in a nunnery'."

"That's right," Ron grinned. "And you can't win. If you try to chat up the nurses, to some you're a budding sex maniac. And if you don't, you're an odd-bod!"

"But, come off it. They can't all have that opinion of us!"

"No, they haven't. But there are some who like to label us in this way."

Bemused, I pursued the matter. "For what reason? Why?"

"Prejudice," answered Ron. "Simple prejudice, but that is their problem, not ours. Now, let's change the subject to something really important. Can we afford another pint between the three of us? Eh?"

Searching out coins from the deepest recesses of our pockets, we contrived the small miracle. And the final, solitary pint was shared between three.

CHAPTER SEVEN
All Sorts of Lessons in the Night

Cockroach Alley was the name we gave to a short cut which led from the main corridor of the hospital to the far side. It was one of a labyrinth of subterranean passages. Twisted, hissing pipes snaked along the walls, but the tentacled things that dropped onto your head, then scuttled into dark recesses, were the real horror.

However, I knew I was late, and this was my first night

on a new ward. Consequently, I sped down the short cut and leapt up the steep stone steps at the far end, panic giving me mountain goat agility.

Finding the door marked 'Night Sister', I knocked, coughed and walked in. The office was unusually large; a tall, thin woman sat at the desk. I took in her scraped-back hairstyle and the facial expression which somehow matched.

"You must be the male nurse," Night Sister announced.

Once again, I felt as if regarded with contempt.

"Now, where can we put him?" Irritable questions were being voiced, but I was quite blatantly ignored. "Where to put him, that's the question!"

Tapping a ballpoint pen against her rather prominent teeth, Night Sister stared at a large board fixed to the wall.

"Aha! It's Simpson Ward for you, my lad. Yes, that's by far the best decision." Still never a glance in my direction. "Report to Simpson Ward, male nurse, as soon as possible. I'll tell them you're on your way."

The Night Sister reached for her telephone, and I, a 'lad' who was fast becoming an old hand at reading body language, took this as dismissal and left the room. I was getting used to members of senior staff who refused to meet the eyes of the young male student who stood, anxious to impress, in front of them.

Musing on the nature of my welcome, I followed a dimly lit corridor. I knew I had been in the presence of Sister Bly, who, it was rumoured, was related to that individual whose cruel obduracy had led to the famous mutiny on the Bounty.

More likely, she was just another representative of the 'Old School', who included male nurses among her list of hates. I would have to tread carefully.

Simpson Ward turned out to be a male orthopaedic

ward of twenty-six beds. The patients looked relatively young. I learned later that road traffic accidents, involving motor cycles in particular, accounted for the presence of many of them.

After rushed introductions made by a Staff Nurse Howard, I was dispatched into the thick of ward activity with a State Enrolled Nurse (SEN) called Croft. In accordance with her qualifications, her uniform was green, of course, not purple. It was characteristic of Nurse Croft to interject into her speech such phrases as, 'Of course, I'm only a *greeny*' or 'Don't ask me, I'm just a *green belt.*' My puzzlement vanished as it became clear that the Nurse's defensive remarks reflected the way many SRN nurses automatically looked down on the SENs. As I worked alongside Nurse Croft, both that night and subsequently, I realised what an excellent, in fact *superior*, nurse she was, and it dawned on me that we few males were not the only objects of prejudice.

As I helped Nurse Croft settle the patients down for the night, I found the medical procedure she was carrying out proved to be an occasion for young males to exhibit certain forms of young male behaviour. As the 'back trolley' visited each curtained-off bed, hugely exaggerated 'Oohs' and 'Aahs' volleyed into the air. On the trolley were soap, surgical spirit and talcum powder. In his turn, each patient presented his bare buttocks, then went through a ritual of ribald remarks.

"Get into bed with me, nurse!" urged one lad, covered with adolescent acne. His plea was followed by screams of laughter from beds up and down the ward.

With her soapy hand, Nurse Croft gave the youth a resounding slap. "What, fancy your mother, do you?" she retorted. "Get another twenty years of experience, and I might consider you!"

Her good-natured snub set off further howls of mirth.

On we went, with our trolley, to the next patient.

"What's the exact purpose of all this?" I gestured towards the trolley's accoutrements.

"What we're doing is stimulating the circulation in the tissues," Nurse Croft explained. "Most of these patients are in traction and are laid on their backs all day, so they're prone to pressure sores."

I looked up and down the ward at all the limbs caught and suspended by weights and pulleys. It was obvious to me now that bums, even youthful bums, would soon get very sore. A few of the patients were older men, some quite elderly. Nurse Croft elaborated on their plight.

"Fractured neck of femur. Very common in the elderly, it is usually caused by a fall. Now, *this* patient's break was so bad he's had to have an artificial head of femur fixed. Isn't that right, Mr Lomas?"

"And bloody painful it is to move, I can tell you." As though to prove the point, the patient shifted the fractured leg and his face registered excruciating pain.

As we carried on down the long ward, Nurse Croft said, "When you come to do theatre, Mike, you'll find orthopaedic surgery's like a carpenter's shop! Hammers, screwdrivers, saws, and the like. And a ruddy battleground it is, I can tell you, with irate surgeons and all. You're in for a real treat, love!"

"Cup of tea, nurses?" enquired a squat little man, wearing a National Health Service dressing gown, and pushing a tea-trolley.

Without once lifting the spout, he filled rows of cups as if wielding a watering can. Fascinated, I watched the liquid spew into the cups.

"No, thank you, Mr Luckerist. We haven't time now; another time, perhaps."

"Your loss, not mine." Shrugging, the patient trundled the trolley on up the ward.

A short while later, the warning, "Lights out!" was shouted by Staff Nurse Howard, just seconds before the ward was plunged into semi-darkness.

The strange twilight effect was further dramatised when the Staff Nurse draped a green dressing towel over the anglepoise lamp on her desk. From this viewpoint all beds could be seen clearly. As Nurse Croft and I sat down, one on each side of her, our faces instantly took on a green hue. We must have looked a grim trio.

The dimming of the lights did not have the desired effect, I noticed. Loud guffaws exploded from the beds as 'dirty' jokes were exchanged, and there was a general loud rustling as patients attempted to get at biscuits in their lockers.

"They're like a set of daft *kids*." Staff Nurse tried to settle down to the reports in front of her.

"The trouble is," Nurse Croft elaborated, "they're not really ill, in the strict sense of the word. They may have broken bones, but that's about it."

"I'd like to break their flaming *necks*." Staff Nurse Howard was angry now, as the noise level showed no signs of abating. She rose to her feet.

"Right! That's it! Enough is enough. Any more of this and I'm sending for Sister Bly."

Just the name did it. At once, the din hushed and, one by one, the lads drifted off. Finally, there was just the sound of snores here and there.

"It's odd being awake, when everyone else is sleeping," I said.

Nurse Croft smiled. "The worst time is from two a.m. onwards. That's when your eyelids seem to have a will of their own."

"Yes, and it's fatal to let them close," said Staff Nurse. "I once found I couldn't open my eyes, or move any part of my body. 'Night nurse's paralysis', they call it!"

In fact, I had heard of this phenomenon: a state akin to

hypnosis, thought to be triggered by extreme fatigue.

"You'd better show Mike how to do obs." Staff Nurse stood up once more, returning her pen to her pocket. "I'll pop down to the office, to take the bed statement."

Suddenly, perhaps encouraged by nocturnal conditions, we were all on first name terms; things were looking up.

'Obs' was revealed as the short-form jargon for 'observations'. This was a method of keeping a check on the ward. It turned out to be extremely tedious work, which consisted of taking blood pressure readings and pulse-rate readings, plus testing pupil of the eye reactions at frequent intervals. The latter procedure involved shining a pencil torch into each eye and noting how it reacted to light. The pupil will normally close on exposure to light, it was explained to me, so failure to close, or an unequal reaction, could denote serious neurological problems, and must be reported immediately.

As Nurse Croft led the way down the ward, she checked several intravenous drips. These, to my novice eyes, were complicated and frightening pieces of apparatus. As the nurse deftly changed bottles of blood, or saline, I marvelled at her confident manner and quiet efficiency.

"This drip will have to be re-sited. Look," she explained as we bent over a sleeping patient. "The drip's run into the tissues."

Now, I could see that the drip had indeed stopped, and that the skin, where the needle had been inserted, was swollen and red.

"Staff Nurse can have a poke about with that later," said Nurse Croft. "I'm only a *greenie*, you see, can't be trusted. Let's get on."

How much I had already learned from this excellent nurse, I reflected. And yet she had become so bitter, so apt to deny her own initiative, due to what was seen as her inferior professional status.

Listening to her self-deprecating remarks taught me a lesson. I determined not to let the attitude of others affect me in this way. I would no longer take the slightest notice of prejudice or hostility in others. I had been too sensitive, too ready to feel inferior when given a hard time. Never again. Nothing must be allowed to turn me bitter.

After we had carried out the observations in a thorough manner, I returned to the lookout post of the desk. As I sat there, suddenly feeling hugely conspicuous, I saw Sister Bly, accompanied by the Staff Nurse, walking down the ward and inspecting each bed. Where was my guide and mentor, Nurse Susan Croft, I wondered uncomfortably, as the two senior staff materialised before me out of the gloom. Casting me a withering look, Sister Bly left the ward with her junior colleague.

When the Staff Nurse returned, she hissed at me in fury, "Mr Bolger, will you kindly find something to do, and not be content with simply sitting at this desk all night. Tidy up the sluice!"

No first names now. The atmosphere had changed, without warning, without apparent justification, to one of volatility. Somehow, I'd blown it. *Bloody hell!*

CHAPTER EIGHT
Trying to Remain Detached

One thirty-five in the morning. Staff Nurse Howard had sent me to the dining room late: evidently, I was still in disgrace.

All the good, hot food had been scoffed, the nurses had gone, and I sat in miserable solitude, chewing on a nauseating mess of cold cauliflower cheese.

This stuff should be sent to Casualty, I mused

mournfully, to help with overdose cases. No need to administer the stomach pump: one look at this and the patient would throw up immediately.

To add to my misery, I registered that, in less than a week, I was to sit my first-year Anatomy and Physiology exam. How the time had flown! Only a few weeks earlier, in 'study block', Miss Grayson had warned us that failure to revise would cost us dearly. With renewed resolution, I promised myself I would get to grips with some serious studying the moment I got off the ward. But a sinking feeling in the gut, made worse no doubt by the glutinous meal, told me things had been left too late. What I didn't know now I would never 'read, mark, learn and inwardly digest' in time for the examination.

One forty-five a.m. I would finish my break in the sitting room, maybe glance at a newspaper, if there was one there. To my surprise, the room was totally dark. Once my eyes adjusted to the gloom, I gawped at the sight of a mass of bodies sprawled over every inch of settee, chair and, indeed, floor. Cloak-covered nurses. They reminded me of a seal colony I had seen on a nature film. Now and then, a figure would stretch, yawn, and then slump back.

As I discovered later, this was an attempt by nurses to snatch perhaps twenty minutes of sleep. My experiment with doing the same revealed that it was a hopeless practice. All this sleep-snatching did was to make you feel, and look, like death for the remainder of the night's duty.

******

"Mike, go with Nurse Croft and prepare an admission bed. *Chop chop!*" Staff Nurse Howard clapped her hands twice. The atmosphere seemed to me to have become less hostile. "We have a suspected spinal injury patient coming up from theatre any minute. He's in a bad way, it seems.

80

Road traffic accident."

At the precise second we finished making up the bed, the ward doors flew open with a crash. The patient, on a trolley, was propelled rapidly towards us.

"This could be tricky," observed Staff Nurse, looking enquiringly at the theatre escort nurse and the porter. "Skeletal traction?"

The escort nurse looked up. She nodded and added sarcastically, "What do you think I'm holding: Scotch mist?"

Sure enough, she had a firm grip on the patient's neck, giving it obvious backward pull. The patient, I now saw, was a young man aged about twenty.

Staff Nurse whispered to us. "The neck's broken and must be kept in constant traction. Failure to do so could result in sudden death."

My eyes fastened on a steel calliper which protruded from both sides of the patient's skull and encircled the head. Attached to this at its centre was a thin wire connected to a series of weights and a pulley. Hardly the moment for levity, but all this life-saving apparatus gave the young man a Frankenstein look.

"Right." Staff Nurse came to a decision. "We must all lift together." On the count of three, the patient was lifted, in forklift truck fashion, as powerfully yet as gently as possible. The pulley was now attached to the bedhead and held in place by a special locking nut. The wire was speedily fed over this and the weights attached. Now, and only now, the escort nurse could relinquish her vital hold on the broken neck.

"Whew!" She rubbed her arm hard. "Am I glad to be shot of that chore! Come on." She beckoned to the porter. "We'll be off."

The patient's eyes looked into mine and held them. "I say, pal, when will I get my feeling back? Tell me it'll come. I'm scared."

"John, isn't it?" Staff Nurse continued briskly, without waiting for confirmation. "It's early days yet. You'll be transferred soon to the spinal injuries unit. They're the real experts in this field. Now, try and relax, love, and get some sleep."

"How the hell can I sleep, when I can't move my arms or legs?" The patient's shout was laced with panic. "When will I get the use back?" Now he was screaming.

"Stay with John, Mike. I'll fetch a sedative."

Staff Nurse now left one very insecure nurse to calm the patient.

"My head feels like a ton weight," he was saying.

"I'm not surprised," I said, adding, "but it's best your head is kept as still as possible for the moment." How sorry I felt for this lad, a chap even younger than myself and facing, did he but know it, a life of wheelchairs and lost opportunities.

In fact, a little later, as we left the sedative to give the lad some respite from his acute and warranted anxiety, I learned that things were even worse than I had guessed.

"This lad's break is very far up the spinal cord," Staff Nurse explained, "so he's quadriplegic, not paraplegic: he's paralysed from mid-chest level, not waist level. His bowels and bladder are affected; he has no use of either organ. He'll have to be turned two-hourly, day and night, to prevent pressure sores."

Appalled, I asked, "Is he likely to regain the use of his limbs at all?"

"It's most unlikely," was the reply, "but not impossible that he might get some use back in time, albeit very limited."

"Sorry to interrupt your teaching session," said Nurse Croft, sarcastically, "but Mr Higgs has still not passed urine since his admission this afternoon."

"Better send for the houseman, Dr Lane, then," replied Staff Nurse. "Meantime, I will show Mike how to set up for a catheterisation."

In the clinical room, various sizes of catheters were selected for use, these being placed on the trolley along with a sterile pack, gloves, 10 ml syringe, sterile water, lignocaine, and a 2,000 ml drainage bag.

Staff Nurse told me a little about the procedure as we pushed the trolley out into the ward.

"Mr Higgs most likely has a prostate problem," she said as we approached the bed.

"Staff Nurse Lomas told me a bit about this, when I was on Lister Ward," I replied.

"Yes, men, from the early age of forty onwards, can be affected by this problem," she said, pushing the trolley in the direction of Mr Higgs. On our arrival, the patient was clearly in some distress.

"Bloody hell, nurse, do something, can't you? I'm busting," he protested. Just then the screens flew back and a white-coated young man, with a pock-marked face, entered the scene.

"I'm Dr Lane," he said. "We'll soon have you more comfortable."

The patient appeared reassured by this and started to relax a little. A cursory examination revealed a grossly distended bladder.

"Not much doubt about that," said Dr Lane, replacing the bedclothes. "Acute retention of urine!"

"I'll leave you with the male nurse, then," said Staff Nurse, obviously eager to be off.

Dr Lane nodded briefly. "I'll just have a word with my colleague," he explained, pulling back the screens, as I dutifully followed him outside. "You've done one of these before?" he enquired, staring at me intently.

"Good God, no!" I exclaimed!

"Well, now is your chance to learn," he said. "There's nothing much to it really. It's simply a matter of shoving a tube into the bladder and inflating a balloon, once in there."

I was sure there was more to it than that, but held my council. After a brief explanation to the patient, who, much to my dismay, gave his permission to act as my guinea pig, I was shown how to catheterise. Dr Lane was an excellent teacher, who guided me through the procedure, step by step, with a good degree of skill. First, draped in sterile sheets, the patient's penis was exposed, and then cleaned, before lignocaine (a local anaesthetic gel) was inserted into the urethra.

"I should leave this about five minutes, before you insert the catheter," advised Dr Lane.

Hands, which trembled slightly, now enclosed in sterile gloves, I started to insert the catheter into the meatus, or opening to the urethra.

"Slowly does it, don't rush it," said Dr Lane, as I gently pushed the catheter further and further along the patient's urethra. "The trick is to insert the catheter up to its fullest length," advised my tutor. "Never guess, over-catheterise every time."

"Why is that?" I asked, still threading the catheter inch by inch into the patient's manhood.

"Because, unless you see urine, there is no real way of knowing for certain that you are in the bladder. If you inflate the balloon in the urethra or bladder neck, you are in big trouble."

Just then, a rush of urine spurted from the catheter.

"Bingo," shouted Dr Lane. "In this case, we have urine, so now you can insert your sterile water into the valve to inflate the balloon."

As requested, I connected a 10 ml syringe to the small appendage at the base of the catheter and slowly inserted the sterile water.

"Now, pull the catheter back out, slowly," came the instructions. "When it stops, you are at the bladder neck."

I felt a certain satisfaction, as the balloon at the catheter tip made contact with the base of the bladder, causing it to stop, as predicted. All that remained was to connect the catheter to the drainage bag, which was now rapidly filling with urine.

"By heck, that feels a damn sight better!" exclaimed the patient, beaming at me, his relief obvious.

"Well done," said Dr Lane. "This is one of the most satisfying procedures you're likely to perform; it brings instant results, see? Well, I'm off."

"Thanks," I said, staring after him. I had learnt a new skill and brought relief to my patient. I felt a warm glow. This was what it was all about: the relief of pain and suffering. I had, in my small way, played a part in this and felt pretty chuffed with myself. But not for long. Suddenly, Croft was at my elbow.

"Come on, snap out of it! Come and help dish out the bowls."

"Already? It's only five o'clock!"

"That's the time we start; never get done otherwise. Can't you hear the dawn chorus?"

Indeed, the sky's inkiness was fading and the first cheeps could be heard.

About to grab the bath trolley for Croft to pile on the bowls, I was distracted by Staff Nurse Howard.

"Never mind about that now! You'd better give me a hand with the injections. God, we'll never get done!"

As I approached, the steriliser at the top of the ward was already boiling and bubbling. Hair damp with steam, Staff Nurse Howard was fishing out the scalding, sterilised syringes and needles and placing them in a kidney dish.

"It's hot, stupid!" exclaimed Staff Nurse, as I almost dropped the scalding kidney dish, with all its freshly sterilised contents. "You've given injections before, I take it?" she queried suspiciously, as she drew up the contents of an ampin of penicillin into a syringe.

"Yes. Yes, I've given injections before." I tried to sound experienced and confident, recalling the javelin-throwing incident of some months earlier.

"Right then," came the response, "get cracking with these." I found myself in the possession of a dish containing three syringes and needles. "Mr Sunderland, bed eleven; Mr Down, bed twelve; and Mr Gibbs, bed twenty. Off you go!"

Mr Sunderland was on traction, his legs suspended by weights. How was I to get to his buttock? My mind was a blank.

"Use the *thigh,* stupid," was the curt advice given in answer to my nervous query.

"By Christ, that was a bit keen," one patient whispered, as I withdrew a syringe. However, it seemed to me that all three patients realised I was a novice and were good enough to make due allowance. For this I was grateful, although it was my own survival of the injection ordeal that impressed me most at that moment.

Nurse Croft bustled back from her own injection extravaganza.

"Help Nurse Croft with the beds now, and do get a move on!"

Most of the patients seemed to accept as normal, indeed inevitable, the frantic early morning ritual of washing and bed-sheet smoothing, as we rushed to be finished by the time the day staff arrived. Not to be ready for the following shift was deemed the crime of all crimes. Wrath would descend on the minutest failure.

"It's worst if you have an early morning death," Nurse Croft elaborated, tightening a bed-sheet. "If the patient dies at eight twenty-nine, one minute before day staff

86

come on, they expect the body to be laid out, sheeted up, ready for the mortuary. No excuses accepted!"

We swooped onto the next bed, scarcely pausing to straighten our spines. "It's us and them, you see, and always will be," she panted.

Night and day staff, like night and day, it seemed, were opposite concepts.

At last, the ward was immaculate. Staff Nurse Howard, flustered and flushed, nevertheless could not find fault with our feverish activity. The ward was a credit to her.

"You two can go," she dismissed, as fresh-eyed nurses walked energetically onto the ward.

Patients, their hair plastered down, their faces scrubbed with a vicious thoroughness, looked at the newcomers with expectancy. Soon they would be exchanging anecdotes on how they had fared during the night and on the state of their symptoms, as they tackled their bowls of porridge and their hard-boiled eggs. They were ready now to face the challenge of a new day. Nurse Croft and I were old news.

"See you tonight, mate. Sleep well!" came a good-natured response to my farewell wave. That was nice.

Hunger, they say, is a good sauce. Never had fried spam and tomatoes tasted so excellent. Mopping up tomato juice with a bread crust, I listened to the talk which ping-ponged around me. Mostly it was shop talk.

"Bly was on the warpath again. She gave me a right blasting," confided a second-year nurse to anyone listening, as she crammed her mouth with bread.

"What for?"

The nurse, blonde and still lively, swallowed her mouthful, and then rose to her feet. Assuming a scarcely exaggerated *grande dame* voice, hands on hips, she mimicked Sister Bly.

"NURSE, when I enter the ward, you stand up IMMEDIATELY! Is that clear? Do you hear me, girl?

87

And take that cardigan off while in my presence! That should have been removed the moment you saw me! Staff Nurse! See to it that this nurse, no matter how ignorant, is made aware of hospital etiquette!"

The act was greeted by shrieks of laughter and wild applause. The nurses evidently felt safe and secure from enemy ears. Now the conversation turned to things clinical. Although weary, my fellow nurses seemed strangely reluctant to let the night go and retire to their soft beds. This was a mixture, I, a shy young male, decided, of adrenaline still flowing and female fondness for talking about everything.

"How's *your* night been?" A friendly little nurse with black hair and a snub nose looked up at me.

"Not bad, really." My grin was unforced. I had realised from the take-off of Sister Bly that my earlier encounter with her had not been as horrendous as it might have been. "Not bad at all," I echoed myself, waves of relief warming me and, shockingly, causing the memory of the tragic young chap, who had looked into my eyes and asked terrible questions, to fade. I had survived yet another spell of duty under the suspicious eyes of the 'old school'.

Not the slightest premonition warned me of an ordeal I was soon to face; an ordeal which would shake me to the core and would result in nightmares for weeks to come.

CHAPTER NINE
A Testing Time All Round

I had already received the official letter from The General Nursing Council for England and Wales, informing me of the date and time of the forthcoming examination. Also enclosed was my personal number, which was to be used in place of my name on all examination papers. No doubt, this was to ensure total impartiality on behalf of the marking examiners. In panic, I threw myself feverishly into an orgy of study, attempting to learn parrot-fashion the nine systems of the body: an impossible task in the allotted time.

"Try this," said Ron, one late afternoon, skimming a small book across my room. *Questions and Answers For Nurses* read the title.

"It's a compilation of recent examination questions with answers," explained Ron. "A kind of concentrated guess at what you may be asked in your exam. It helped me. May help you," he said, slouching out of the room, hands in pockets.

The book, written by tutors who were ex-GNC examiners, obviously had some merit. I picked it up and read avidly.

'What are the functions of the skeleton? Enumerate its contents,' read the first question.

'The skeleton provides a movable framework for the rest of the body,' ran the answer, then went onto describe the various bones in detailed sequence. The book was good. In fact, it was a Godsend. Not only did it give valuable information, but gave the type and style of answers the examiners were looking for. I decided on a gamble: abandon the approved, standard textbook of the day and go for this small, concentrated version.

Ron, as usual, gave sound advice.

"The little book is fine, if used in the proper context," he said. "You will have gained far more knowledge than you think. Simply use the book to back this up. One further piece of advice I would give," he added. "Don't study to the bitter end. What you don't know the day before the exam, you'll never know."

I took his advice literally. On the eve of the fateful day, I took a course of Dutch courage at the local pub. As I reached for my third, and what I thought was my last pint, things were looking distinctly more cheery.

"You'll walk it," said Dave convincingly, already a pint ahead of me.

"Of course he will," agreed Tony, looking first at me, then at his empty glass.

"One more all round," said Ron, getting to his feet.

"No," I protested. "I can't risk a hangover in the morning."

"Shut up and get this down you," said Ron, slamming a pint down in front of me. "This will give you the sleep of the innocent tonight."

"Bloody hell, that is stretching things a bit far," laughed Tony. "Mind you, come to think of it, you always did say we were like monks in a nunnery!"

The day of the exam dawned fresh and sunny. Luckily for me, the day coincided with my nights off, no quarter being given to those unfortunate souls not so blessed. The examination was held in The School of Nursing, at ten a.m. prompt. All the group were there on my arrival.

"I shall fail," wailed Sonya.

"So will I," wailed Mary Platts.

"Oh, shut up," I said. "If anybody fails, it's sure to be me!"

"That's OK then," they both laughed. "You've convinced us."

All the group then suffered from an endemic increase in frequency of micturition until summoned into the exam room by a stern-faced invigilator.

On each desk, face down, lay a threatening-looking, vivid yellow-coloured exam paper. We all chose a desk, then sat waiting apprehensively for the invigilator, who now strolled slowly but deliberately to the head of the room. She was a hatchet-faced woman of about fifty, dressed in black, with beady eyes of the same colour. She reminded me of a crow.

"You will turn your exam papers over when I give the word," she said, in a voice surprisingly softer than her features. "You are expected to answer five questions out of seven in the allotted time. For those non-mathematicians among you, that is half an hour per question. I will remind you when time is up, ten minutes before the end of the exam. Please use your personal number at the head of each sheet and not your name. This would disqualify you. You may turn your paper over now, and good luck."

I turned over the bilious-looking paper with shaking hands, not daring to look down at the questions below. At the top of the paper were the names of the examiners, while below, in larger print, was stated:

PRELIMINARY STATE EXAMINATION - PART 1.

Tuesday, 1st October, 1963.
ELEMENTARY ANATOMY & PHYSIOLOGY and
PERSONAL & COMMUNAL HEALTH.
Time allowed 2½ hours.

IMPORTANT - <u>Read</u> the questions <u>carefully</u>, and <u>answer only what is</u> <u>asked,</u> as no marks will be given for irrelevant matter.

I eventually steeled myself, darting a quick look at the questions. God! I thought, perusing the list, I can't answer any of these! Then, suddenly, a question appeared to leap off the page! 'What are the functions of the skeletal system? Describe the gross structure of a typical long bone. What foods are important in the formation of healthy bone?' What luck! At least I could answer one! With a sense of euphoria, pen in hand, I started to write.

Towards the end of the first question, I glanced at the

remainder and decided next on: 'Name the parts of the brain, and describe its protective covering.' This left me with a further two anatomy questions to answer, there being only one on hygiene. I was not as sure of these remaining questions, but being able to answer the first had at least given a boost to my flagging ego. I answered these to the best of my ability and struggled gamely on.

"Ten more minutes left to complete your paper," came the softly spoken warning.

Surely, time couldn't be up already, I thought, in panic. Only halfway through the communal health question, I was grappling with the intricacies of the dangers of drinking impure water and how to make safe the water supply of a big city.

"Finish writing now, please." This time the voice was louder and more authoritative than before, compelling me to throw down my pen with a sigh.

Joining the group outside, the general consensus of all was that everyone had failed. Even the brightest among us bewailed this fact, which was daft really, as I knew at least two of the girls had an A level in biology. Everyone was now talking excitedly at once.

"What a foul paper. I couldn't answer one question," remarked a girl I had observed scribbling furiously the length of the exam.

"How did you get on, Mike?" The question came from a tall, willowy girl called Jean Lomax.

"I really don't know," I said. "Time will tell, I suppose."

"Indeed it will," she said, with a smile. "It's funny to think we're already in our second year. Don't forget to visit the sewing room to get your second stripe when you get your results."

"I won't," I said, with a laugh. God, I thought, we've all nearly made corporal at last!

******

"You're to report to Flemming Ward tonight, male nurse," said Sister Bly, as I attempted to slide surreptitiously past her office door. "Well, don't stand there gaping, man. Get a move on. Nurse Coggin is expecting you."

Bloody hell, I thought. No explanations, no consideration. Flemming Ward I knew was a male medical unit, a field I knew precious little about. The ward was in the basement and I descended the steps reluctantly, but with reasonable haste. On entering the double doors, which appeared to be made of a kind of black floppy rubber, I was greeted by a tall, thickset girl, wearing horn-rimmed spectacles, who I took to be Nurse Coggin.

"Oh, no, not a bloody male. That's all I need. Have you seen what Bly has landed us with?"

This remark was proffered to a crafty-looking auxiliary with a face like a ferret, who, by way of reply, simply raised her eyes to heaven.

"You go and settle the patients down for the night with Mrs Evans, while I take the report," said Nurse Coggin.

Obviously, I was to be excluded from the presence of the Day Sister, who, later on, I observed placing a sympathetic arm on that of Nurse Coggin before leaving the ward. I must not become paranoid, I told myself, between gritted teeth, as I carried gamely on, settling the patients for the night with the obnoxious Mrs Evans. My auxiliary colleague was by this time hell-bent on finding out as much as she could about me, no doubt eager to discover any titbit of scandal for her colleague. What was the last ward I had worked on? Was I married? Had I a girlfriend? As I replied to each of her questions, her eyelids flickered slyly, as though savouring each answer for her own interpretation. Hell, I *was* becoming paranoid! I discovered later, however, that my instincts were correct. Mrs Evans was not only the biggest gossip of the hospital, she thrived on it.

The patients, I discovered, were all pretty ill, unlike the ones on my previous ward. Most appeared to be suffering from heart problems, although there was a scattering of diabetics, chest complaints, gastric ulcers, and various blood disorders.

"Have you ever passed a Ryle's tube? A nasogastric tube, then?" This question was asked of me by an exasperated Nurse Coggin.

"No," was my simple answer.

My senior raised her eyes to the heavens.

"Well, you'll bloody well have to learn and damn fast, I can tell you! I have five milk drips to set up and I don't intend setting them up on my own," came her caustic reply.

"What are milk drips?" I asked, completely baffled.

"Mr Lloyd, the consultant of this ward, favours milk drips for his gastric ulcer patients," explained Nurse Coggin. "The reason behind this is to prevent the build-up of acid in the stomach. As you may be aware, it is thought that most gastric ulcer patients secrete too much acid. This excess helps create the formation of ulcers by inflaming sections of the stomach lining."

"Ah, so our milk drips give the acid something to feed on, thus protecting the ulcer," I proffered.

"God, it actually thinks," exclaimed Nurse Coggin, in mock amazement.

"Yes," I replied with equal sarcasm, "and a mere male at that. Isn't that incredible?"

To my surprise, her face broke into a grin.

"Ah, decided to fight back at last," she said. "I wondered how long it would take."

The method soon became clear to me. Milk was first brought to the boil in a large pan then left to cool. To this was added a measure of Aludrox, a kind of alkaline peppermint suspension. Next, with the aid of a funnel, the mixture was poured into large Winchester-type bottles. A large rubber bung was inserted into the top of each bottle, into which was pushed a large, needle-like rod. To this was connected a length of rubber tubing, holding in its midst a clear glass phial and gate clip, thus enabling one to regulate the speed, or rate, of drip when connected to the patient's nasogastric tube. Each bottle had at its base a metal clip enabling it to be suspended from a drip stand. That was the easy bit. Next came the passing of five nasogastric tubes. I watched intently as Nurse Coggin demonstrated how simple this was, by giving a running commentary.

"Come on, Mr Woodhouse. You've done this many times before," she said, as we approached a very apprehensive-looking man in scarlet red pyjamas. "We first dip the end of the tube in a little liquid paraffin. We then insert the tube up the nostril, like this, then get the patient to swallow as the tube passes down the back of the throat. Good man, Mr Woodhouse. That's it," she coaxed. "Swallow, swallow."

To my inexperienced eye, all appeared to be going well. That was until the patient suddenly grabbed hold of the tube and yanked it out. His face blended perfectly with his pyjamas, chameleon-like. He looked every inch the angry reptile!

"Mr Woodhouse, why have you done that?" said an exasperated Nurse Coggin.

The patient was obviously in no mood for compromise.

"Bugger off, the pair of you! Get the hell out of it!" he yelled.

Beating a hasty retreat, we made for the clinical room.

Nurse Coggin was furious, not so much with the patient, but because she had lost face in front of me. Full of venom, she attempted to save what was left of her dignity by snarling at me.

"Well, don't just stand there, gaping like an idiot," she spat. "Bring the drip stand and let's get on."

Mercifully, the next two patients were more co-operative, the fine red tubes appearing to glide effortlessly down their gullets. I watched her connect a syringe to the end of the tube and aspirate a clear, grey liquid, which I took to be gastric contents. This was then tested on blue litmus paper, which immediately turned pink. *Blue to pink equals acid, I think; pink to blue, alkaline true*, I thought, suddenly remembering the little ditty Miss Grayson taught us.

"You always do this test, to make sure the tube is in the stomach and not the lungs," explained Nurse Coggin. "Now, let's see how you perform."

To my relief, the next patient was an old hand at this, practically performing the whole procedure on his own.

"I've missed my vocation," he said with a grin. "I ought to have been a sword-swallower."

"What's this?" said Nurse Coggin, as I pulled the drip stand towards the bed. "Where did you get that tubing from?"

While setting up the equipment earlier, I had realised there was insufficient tubing, and had been told to improvise by my irate colleague. Seeing several intravenous transfusion boxes, I had done just that.

"I've used a giving set," I replied.

Receiving little response to this, I assumed I had done something right at last. Soon all four milk drips were on the go. We decided to leave the angry chameleon to his slumbers.

The remainder of the night passed without incident and ended with the usual early waking routine of bowls, bowels, injections and medications. Nurse Coggin remained sulkily hostile to the end, spending the quieter moments of the night in whispered conversation with Mrs Evans. It was, therefore, one very thankful male nurse who left for the sanctuary of his bed that morning, blissfully unaware of the troubles ahead.

******

To say I was pleased to be back on good old Simpson Ward the following night would be to state the obvious.

"How did you find Flemming Ward?" asked Staff Nurse Howard. "As bad as that, eh?" she said, reading my face.

"What did you expect?" laughed Nurse Croft. "Don't you know who he was working with?"

"No," replied Staff Nurse. "Who?"

"Clever Clogs Coggin, no less!"

"Bloody hell, no wonder he looks so dejected. She's an absolute cow, that one," she said with a laugh, as she turned to answer the telephone. Her face suddenly lost all semblance of humour, as she replied, "Yes. Right away, Sister. I'll tell him. Mike, that was Bly. You've to report to the Day Sister on Flemming Ward, immediately! What have you done?"

"Christ knows, but I have a feeling I'm soon going to find out," I said, my stomach suddenly starting to sink.

"Good luck," they both said, looking genuinely concerned.

I knew a little about the Sister I was about to meet. Dave had worked for her for a while and found her to be OK. In fact, he said, she liked a laugh and was certainly not anti-male.

"What's that?"

I followed Sister Glover's eyes to the empty giving set

box on her desk and stated the obvious.

"It's a giving set, Sister."

"I am well aware of that fact," she hissed with stiffening back. She was a very attractive woman, in her mid-thirties, with a nice figure; pretty and quite fanciable under different circumstances, I mused, but not now! The tirade continued. "How dare you use an intravenous giving set as a milk drip on my ward!" she went on, not giving me time to speak. "If there had been a serious haemorrhage on this ward, there could have been serious consequences. You could have been held responsible. Is there any reason why I should not report you to Matron?"

That there were five spare giving sets in the clinical room appeared not to matter. It was obvious Coggin was at the back of this. I decided not to argue the point, but try a little flattery and play the helpless male.

"I'm sorry, Sister. I'm finding it difficult to concentrate. That scent. It isn't 'Entice' by any chance, is it?"

Sister Glover looked at me incredulously. "Don't you dare to patronise me," she said, but as our eyes met I could see the slightest hint of amusement in hers. "As a matter of fact, it is 'Entice', but flattery will get you absolutely nowhere," she remarked.

"It was worth a try, Sister," I said, "but I really do like that particular brand of perfume, honestly."

She suddenly laughed.

"You're a cheeky beggar, I'll grant you that. Go on, clear off out of my sight, before I change my mind about reporting you."

I needed no second bidding and shot out of the office like a cork from a bottle. As I emerged, I spied Nurse Coggin, who had obviously been listening at the door. With great deliberation, I put my hand to my mouth and blew her a kiss. The look that followed me from the ward is best not described. Being a male could have its advantages after all!

******

My spell on night duty appeared to be speeding along at a breakneck pace. The term 'all bed and work' was now becoming totally familiar to me as day merged into night and night into day, in monotonous succession. Working a forty-eight hour week gave me just two nights off in seven. I seemed to exist in a totally different world, but was becoming more familiar with the routine and starting to enjoy the slight increase in responsibility. Much to my joy, I had passed my 'Part 1' nursing exam, but was sad to learn that three of the group had failed. It was now, just as I was feeling more comfortable with my nursing colleagues and much more settled, that the bombshell fell!

"Mike, I've just seen your name on the change list," said Nurse Croft, bounding onto the ward early one evening.

"It can't be," I said, aghast. "I've only been on nights three months!"

"Nearly four, Mike," Nurse Croft corrected. "You've obviously lost track of time, old son."

"Where am I for?" I asked, now truly alarmed.

"Theatre, and the best of luck," replied Croft, who was now thoroughly enjoying herself.

Theatre! The very name stuck terror! I knew full well this was no bed of roses. The theatre Sister had a reputation second to none and was legendary for her strict regime and hard taskmaster approach. She definitely did not suffer fools gladly!

"What's up with old misery guts?" said Staff Nurse Howard, suddenly spying my melancholic expression.

"Theatre," I said.

"Ah well, all good things come to an end, I suppose. You'll come through it. I did," said Staff Nurse. "You will certainly need your wits about you. You may get the odd telling-off from Sister, but I'll say one thing for her: she doesn't bear grudges and has never sent anyone to Matron – not yet anyway!"

During the early hours of that morning the silence of the ward was shattered by the shrill sound of the office phone.

"We're not on take, are we, Mike?" asked Staff Nurse, a puzzled expression on her face.

"Not that I'm aware," I replied, as she made her way to the office.

It was unusual for the phone to ring at this hour unless something really urgent was afoot.

"Mike, it's Bly for you," hissed Staff Nurse. "Look lively. You know she doesn't like to be kept waiting!"

With the now-familiar sinking feeling in the pit of my stomach, I rose to my feet and followed her into the office. Staff Nurse handed me the receiver with a grimace, then stood watching, as I said a cautious, "Hello?"

There was no return of greeting from the other end, simply instructions.

"Male nurse, the night porter has taken ill and his relief has not yet arrived. There is a body to remove. You will collect the mortuary trolley from outside the laundry and meet me on Nightingale Ward!"

Then the receiver was replaced.

"What on earth is it?" said Staff Nurse, alarmed by my facial expression.

"I have to take a body to the mortuary," I said, with a gulp.

"You won't be on your own. You'll have Bly for company," she replied.

"I think I'd prefer just the corpse!" I said, attempting

to bring a bit of levity into the proceedings.

I bumped into Nurse Croft, on my way out.

"Where are you off to at this hour?" she enquired, obviously puzzled.

"Don't even ask," I said, heading with all haste towards the laundry.

A few minutes later saw me trundling the mortuary trolley along the corridor towards Nightingale Ward. It resembled a large, hinged, grey, oblong box on wheels and it gave me the creeps.

Sister Bly was waiting for me as I arrived, hovering about impatiently at the ward door.

"Ah, there you are at long last. What kept you?" she snapped. Not waiting for a reply, she said, "The side ward and don't make a noise!"

I pushed the trolley alongside the screened-off bed and stared down at the white-sheeted corpse in front of me.

"You take the top end, I'll take the bottom," whispered Bly, as I opened up the box. The subdued lighting cast an eerie glow over the proceedings, as we slowly slid the body onto the trolley and closed the lid.

"Get this bed stripped and washed in carbolic immediately, nurse," ordered Bly, as we pushed the trolley out into the corridor. The ward nurse nodded dumbly in reply, as Bly and I headed off towards the rear of the hospital with our grim cargo.

There being no moon, the night was inky black, as we emerged from the back of the boiler house and made our way across an open space of yard towards our macabre destination. The mortuary, or Rose Cottage, as it was sometimes referred to, was a large, single, flat-roofed building with frosted glass windows. At this moment in time, it looked to me about as cheerful as Count Dracula's castle. In fact, had I the choice, I would have gladly preferred the latter.

"There's usually a light on in this area," whispered Bly. "Must remember to report it."

Two large double doors now faced us. Sister Bly handed me her torch, then, fumbling with a large key, she finally inserted it into the lock.

"That's odd!" she exclaimed. "The key is turning in the lock, but the door won't open! There is obviously something lodged at the back of the door."

"What do we do now?" I asked. "Return to the ward?"

"Can't do that, male nurse," she replied. "Wouldn't be ethical. You wait here. I won't be a minute."

She disappeared round the other side of the building, leaving me literally in the dark. She returned soon after, her face ghastly but jubilant in the glow of her torch.

"I have the answer," she said, obviously pleased with herself. Not waiting for a reply she outlined her plan.

"What a stroke of luck! I found one of the post-mortem

room windows open. The solution is obvious. You will enter by this route and open the door from the inside."

Suddenly, the hairs at the back of my neck appeared to take on a will of their own.

"You can't be serious, Sister," I implored. "It's pitch black in there."

"Nonsense," she replied. "Here, take my torch. Now let's get on with it! You can stand on the trolley to reach the window."

As though in a dream, I pushed the trolley round the back of the building, stopping just below a half-open window. The whole episode now had all the qualities of a first-class nightmare. I scrambled on top of the trolley and shone my torch through the open window. A row of six stainless steel post-mortem tables gleamed coldly in the reflected light. I was grateful that at least none had an occupant.

"Do get on," hissed Bly, as I cocked a leg through the open window top.

Perching on a small ledge inside, I launched myself into space. I had unfortunately failed to see a small instrument cabinet parked directly beneath my entrance. My heels caught on it. With a yell, I went base over apex onto the floor with a bang. The torch somersaulted out of my hand, landed, then flickered a couple of times before going out.

As I sat there in the dark, the silence was deafening. All that could be heard was the solitary drip, drip of a tap. Telling myself not to panic, I rose to my feet and groped my way slowly forward. I was always scared of the dark as a child, but this was something else. God, I was scared!

My eyes were slowly getting accustomed to the dark and I now made out the outline of a door. I knew this would lead me to freedom, but at a cost. First I had to pass through the area where the bodies were stored. Opening the door slowly, I stepped into a larger room. Through the

104

gloom I could make out rows of white, name-plated doors. I gave a gulp. Fridges! It was then that I spied the answer to the blocked door. A large plank lay against a set of double doors, wedged beneath a cross-beam.

"Is that you, male nurse?"

Never had Sister Bly sounded so good. I could have kissed her. Starting to relax a little now, I made to remove the wooden plank obstructing the door. It was then that it happened!

From behind, out of the still blackness, came a sudden whirring rushing sound, followed by a sudden loud shudder! Something evil was coming out of the dark to get me! With a cry of terror, I tore blindly at the plank, falling on all fours as the door burst open. I found myself looking up at Sister Bly.

"What on earth's the matter with you, man? You look as if you've seen a ghost."

"I think I have," I said, telling her of the noise from hell. It was the first and only time I was to hear Bly laugh.

"That noise was the result of the fridge thermostat turning on," she explained. "The fridges are all new. The sound was purely vibratory."

CHAPTER TEN
Life Could Have Been Worse

I was in buoyant mood, with a week's holiday and a 'gig' to look forward to. Hospital worries were now far from my mind. I had, after many lessons painfully learnt and paid for, acquired a second-hand drum kit, on credit, and joined a local rock group. The members consisted of: Harry, an asthmatic, Elvis-lookalike vocalist; Johnny, lead guitar; Carl, rhythm guitar; Frank on sax; Alan, double bass; and, of course, yours truly on drums.

I had, like a lot of teenagers who grew up in the fifties and 'swinging' sixties, been excited by the rhythm of Lonnie Donnigan and his skiffle group. Like many others, I obtained an old tea chest, in the centre of which I had fixed an old broom handle. To the broom handle I affixed one taut length of string. Placing a foot on the chest for stability, one could, by stretching and plucking the string, create a sound similar to a double bass. If a tea chest was unattainable, all that was required was a scrubbing board and a set of thimbles to make the other, equally important, rhythmical accompaniment to the skiffle sound. But for me, it was Bill Haley and The Comets that really captured the music scene, with 'Rock Around The Clock', the theme music to the film *The Blackboard Jungle*.

As a rock drummer, one really had to master two things: the drum roll and something called the 'rim shot'. The latter consisted of hitting the side of the snare drum and skin at the same time, thus giving the familiar hollow, sharp snap, so characteristic of the rock beat. The drum roll, on the other hand, took hours of practice to perfect. Unless the drummer was using a practice pad, it was guaranteed to send anyone in the vicinity crackers.

Our first booking was at The Laycock Engineering Sports Club, Sheffield. That first Saturday night saw me eagerly setting up my kit on the small raised stage in the corner of the room. Base drum with foot pedal, snare drum, tom-toms, high hat (foot cymbals), and large cymbal all assembled, I sat, with mounting excitement, watching the steady influx of teenagers. Was it my imagination, or were some of the girls giving me the eye as I tried out a few practice rim shots on the well-worn skins of the kit?

Eventually, after much chord strumming, tuning up, with the odd high-pitched squeak from the sax player, all appeared ready. Then Harry, adding a touch of drama to the proceedings, suddenly leapt on stage, grabbed the hand mike, which he deftly threw from one hand to the other, before launching into the Elvis classic 'Don't Step on My Blue Suede Shoes'. This was quickly followed by 'Jail House Rock', which brought the house down. That applause was elixir to our ears as Harry, flushed with success and wheezing slightly, turned and whispered, "Peggy Sue." Now 'Peggy Sue' is a drummer's delight, or nightmare, consisting, as it does, completely of drum roll. That roll had to be even throughout, just like an electric buzzer, and I trembled slightly, sticks in hand, waiting in anticipation for Harry to kick off.

"I love you, Peggy Sue, With a love so rare and true, My Peggy, my Peggy Sue hoo, hoo, hoo, Oh, I love you gal, I love my Peggy Sue," sang Harry, as I alternated the drum roll tone for maximum effect.

Girls twirled like spinning tops, while the lads appeared to stand on one spot, content to pull and push their partners round, with the odd bit of foot movement and the minimum of effort.

Again, we ended to tumultuous applause from our young audience. Sticks in hand, I wiped the sweat from my eyes, wallowing in the sudden surge of adrenaline brought on by the unexpected, ego-boosting adoration. This was an absolute tonic for me, so different from the hospital scene, where my ego so often appeared to hit rock bottom. There was no doubt about it: the group was good. We had played well, were appreciated, and it felt bloody good! Cliff Richard, eat your heart out, I thought, later that evening, when a couple of teeny-boppers shyly asked for my autograph, as I dismantled my kit.

******

What a contrast! From the theatre of stage to the theatre of surgery! Now, dressed in green smock, green trousers and white boots, I stood about, looking and feeling every inch the spare bridesmaid at the wedding. I had been given a whistle-stop tour of the theatre suite earlier that morning by a sullen-faced State Enrolled Nurse called Dixon. Staring at me through her over-large spectacles, she gave a hasty commentary as we moved rapidly through the department.

"This is the anaesthetic room," she said proudly, pausing briefly. "I work in here, assisting the anaesthetist."

"That must be a responsible job," I said, eager to make an impression with a little flattery.

"You must be joking. The only thing Dixon is any good at is making tea!"

This remark was proffered by a cheeky-looking lad in a white coat, whom I took to straight away.

"Mark is the name," he said, shaking me by the hand in a hearty grip.

"This is the theatre porter," said Dixon, giving Mark a contemptuous look. "I would advise you to stay well clear of him if you want to avoid trouble."

"You know you love me really," said Mark, wrinkling up his nose in mock affection.

"Oh, get out of my way," said Dixon, clearly annoyed by his infringement of her authority.

I entered the operating theatre proper and give an inward gasp as I took in the drama of it all. The theatre table was centre stage, standing, as it did, directly beneath a massive operating lamp. A circle of green, sterile-sheeted trolleys, standing as through silently waiting to serve surrounded it. Against the far wall stood a metal frame made up of numbered pegs, used for counting swabs. To one side of this, through screened off windows, I spied a row of sinks and high levered taps: obviously the scrub room.

"This is the sterilising room," said Dixon, taking me into an offshoot of the main theatre, where two massive sterilises hissed furiously, sending great gouts of steam.

"All the instruments are boiled in here before surgery. I expect Sister will go through the general set with you before long," she said. Seeing my puzzled look, she explained further. "The general set is a standard set of instruments made up of scalpels, retractors, artery forceps and the like, you will be expected to learn these off by heart.

You see, other instruments are added to these as required, as, for example, in orthopaedic or thoracic surgery, but the general set never alters and always remains the same. A word of warning. Try and keep out of Sister's way if you can. She can be a bit keen first thing. Mellows a bit later on, though. She's strict but fair – her responsibilities weigh heavy at times which makes her sharp but her bark's worse than her bite really."

With this cursory warning, she abandoned me, slipping deftly across to the opposite side of the room to join a group of green-attired colleagues.

I stood about, feeling ill at ease, when suddenly a door banged open and in crashed an extremely tall, but stocky woman in theatre greens, her face badly scarred from a previous road traffic accident, which had left her with only one eye – the wearing of a black eye patch did little to enhance her look of severity. I could have imagined her serving with her colleague aboard the HMS Bounty! This, however, did not impair her in any way; she was as sharp as a razor and missed nothing. This must be the boss lady, Sister Flint, I guessed. Was it my imagination or did all the staff appear to be more on their toes with conversation more subdued, more whispered.

Surgeons were scrubbing up as the first listed patient arrived. He was lifted unconscious onto the table, with the aid of canvas sheet and poles.

"Here, you - yes, you. Hold this leg up while I connect to the diathermy machine."

These instructions were given to me by a fresh-faced theatre technician called Lomas. A damp pad was applied to the patient's upper thigh, which in turn was covered by a thin metal plate, from which ran leads to a machine about the size of a small fridge.

"Stops bleeding, old chap, before blood vessels are released," explained Lomas.

"A press on this pedal and a touch of the lead against the artery forceps and, zap, the vessel is sealed."

The anaesthetist, seated with his apparatus at the head end of the table, gave a go ahead nod to the approaching surgeon, who, was still having his gown tied as he walked in, held out his hand to the scrub nurse.

The exposed abdomen was first wiped with iodine, and now took on a brownish hue. The surgeon slung the swab forceps on the floor before taking up his scalpel. This was the first time I had seen an operation, so I craned my neck forward, standing on tiptoe in order to get a better view. A Thin red line followed the scalpel incision, which opened out to reveal yellow fat, then muscle layer, as the surgeon entered the peritoneal, or abdominal, cavity. Blood vessels were clamped and retractors applied before the patient's intestines were brought out onto the surface and spread about like so many links of pork sausages. The surgeon absentmindedly threaded these through his fingers as he engaged in some light-hearted banter with his senior registrar.

"Saw you at the golf club the other day, Rupert. Didn't have time to chat, old man. Valerie was a bit of flap; damm bridge club of hers."

"That's ok, Charles. Quite understand. Had a lousy round, actually. Made up for it later, though, with the aid of the old amber liquid, what! Haw, haw, haw."

This good-humoured banter seemed oddly out of place in this tense situation. Suddenly the frivolity ceased.

"Just a minute. What's this?" The consultant stopped as a black and necrotic-looking section of gut came into view.

"Ah, this is the cause of the problem. Look, Rupert, a

simple enough obstruction. We'll anastomose, and then come out. How is he doing, Bob? All right your end?"

A nod from the anaesthetist confirmed all was well. So, the offending section of gut was removed and the two ends sutured together. Then, with amazing dexterity and a kind of careless abandon, the surgeon pushed the exposed gut back from whence it came.

"I'll leave you to close up, Rupert. Want to nip onto Lister Ward to look at a burst abdomen."

"On your way," said his colleague, obviously pleased to be trusted by his senior. Little wisps of smoke gave evidence of sealed vessels, as artery forceps were released.

"Swab count, please, Sister, before we close," requested the registrar.

"Fifteen," snapped the scrub nurse, counting her remaining swabs before glancing at the rack, clearly annoyed that the senior registrar hadn't even noticed her or the rank she carried.

I was so engrossed in all the happenings, I didn't see a menacing figure approaching my rear. A sudden sharp poke in the back made me spin round.

"Oh, you are alive then, not just part of the furniture?"

I gulped hard. It was Flint, and she looked very angry.

"We get our sleeves rolled up in this department, young man. We don't just stand about. I will tell you when you can observe. I have just the job for you. You see the numbered pegs on this rack? See those long forceps? Well, when the surgeon drops a swab, you pick it up and place it on a peg. Think you can manage that?"

I groaned inwardly. Only a few hours in theatre and perhaps I was already in the doghouse.

The rest of the day saw me crawling about on all fours, picking up blood-soaked swabs, which had been aimed at the bucket but usually landed on the floor. The most exasperating thing was to have a swab clearly in my sights and make a move to retrieve it, only to be thwarted by a surgeon's boot. This swab usually stuck firmly to the sole. I then had to crawl after the moving boot, in the hope of removing it before the final swab count. The list of operations appeared never-ending: as one patient went out, another came in. Lunch brought a temporary respite to the proceedings and I was glad of the company of Mark, the theatre porter.

"I can't give you any comfort, Mike," he said. "You have to learn damn quickly in this department. You're bound to make mistakes; I should know, I make them often enough." With this, he offered his hand. "Join the club," he said with a grin.

"I shall expect you to know these off by heart, male nurse," said Flint, as I stared dumbfounded at the tray laid out before me. "I shall repeat this once and once only," she said, rattling off the names of the various instruments without pausing for breath. "That completes the general set. Woe betide you, if you forget!" But before she stormed off, I already had.

Some three weeks later saw me scrubbed up for an appendectomy, my first case. I was especially nervous, due to the fact that the surgeon I was assisting was the same one who had thrown me out of theatre over the lamp incident. He was a pompous surgeon by the name of Charles Parker-Nobbs and as keen as mustard.

"What have we here, Sister? You know I prefer a pretty little thing to assist me, not one of these male nurse fellows."

"I know, sir, but please bear with us. They have to be trained, you see."

"I know that, sister," he said, peeling off his gloves,

"But I think I'll sit this one out".

"Lady Luck was with me this day," I thought as his Registrar gave me a sly wink. I was talked through the three operations listed, any instruments I was unsure of being pointed out by the good-natured surgeon. However, this was not missed by the sharp-eyed Sister Flint who at the end of the proceedings hissed ...

"I told you to learn the general set!"

"You had better learn and damn quick. It's nights for you in a few weeks, my lad. Yes, you will be in sole charge, so look learn and listen. Now is the acceptable time!"

******

Night duty was a different ball game altogether. It was amazing to think that after only minimal experience, I was, as threatened, now responsible for anything that came in. The remainder of the previous week saw me scrubbed up for a circumcision and a haemorrhoidectomy - hardly major surgery. I also had a taste of orthopaedic surgery, being given the dubious privilege of holding a leg steady during an amputation. Once severed, I suddenly realised the limb was now my responsibility. It felt amazingly heavy in my arms as I moved away from the table. I stood, feeling ridiculous and conspicuous, not knowing what to do with it or where to put it. Luckily, Lomas, the theatre technician, seeing my predicament, took pity on me and relieved me of my macabre load.

The theatre at night was as quiet as the proverbial morgue, but this was to be no cushy number. A stack of chores left by Sister Flint awaited me on my arrival and included the packing of a host of drums for the autoclave steriliser. Each drum had to be packed with a variety of different dressing packs, a most complicated procedure, given the fact that I knew little of what many of these specialist-type dressings looked like. Although a large book contained instructions on how each drum should be filled, my ignorance made this, at best, pure guesswork. I shuddered at the thought of an irate Flint opening one of these the following week, and prayed I would be off duty when this occurred. After the drums came the gloves, hundreds of the things, washed and hung to dry. These had to be blown out, so that the fingers did not adhere together, then placed palm upwards, with a gauze-filled talcum ball, before being slotted into cloth pockets marked left and right. Next came the instruments. These had to be removed from their respective cabinets and cleaned with methylated spirits before being replaced exactly as found.

To say that I lived in constant dread of the theatre telephone during those lonely hours would be to state the obvious. I became almost phobic. The lads of Wellgate Mount did their best to allay my fears, reassuring me that only the odd appendix was likely to adorn my table, with a nice friendly registrar to perform the surgery. Imagine my total panic when the phone rang one night. The voice on the other end was Dr Dutt. No one could mistake his polite but obvious Indian accent.

"You are expecting a fracture of the pelvis, my friend," came the melodious voice. "There are suspected internal injuries also, probably a ruptured bladder. Can you be pleased to be setting up straight away?"

"Who is doing the operation?" I asked, my mouth now resembling the inside of a Japanese wrestler's jock strap.

"Mr Charles Parker-Nobbs, of course. Please to be expecting him in half an hour."

The exclamation I made rhymed with 'clucking bell', as I stood rooted to the spot in pure unadulterated panic. Then all hell broke loose, as I rushed about like something demented. First I phoned Bly to ask for a relief nurse, before turning the sterilisers on full belt, and setting up two trolleys with everything, including the kitchen sink.

"Well, where are they?" The relief nurse glared at her

watch, then at me. She was truly not amused.

"I can't understand it. It's almost an hour gone," I said, totally perplexed.

Just then, the phone rang.

"It's for you," said the stony-faced relief nurse, handing me the receiver.

"It is cancelled, my friend," came the familiar voice.

"Was it a fatality?" I asked, guilty at feeling so relieved.

"No, my friend," said the softly spoken voice, "we discovered it was wrongly diagnosed. It was simply an acute attack of flatus."

"*Flatus?* You must be kidding!" I exclaimed.

"No, my friend. Listen." The sound of a loud raspberry, followed by background screams of laughter, issued from the receiver.

"You set of bastards," I said. "I'll get you for this."

They were still blowing raspberries as I put the phone down.

My spell of nights at an end, saw me back on days once more, where I became quickly embroiled in trouble. "What shall I do with this?" asked a nurse newly arrived in theatre during a particularly hectic day. Everyone appeared busy, pushed to the limit, tempers short. Glancing quickly at the instrument in her hand I observed it was long, tube like and of stainless steel. "Boil it," I said, thinking this by far the safest option. Then, quickly dismissing the incident from my mind, I went about my duties.

The following morning saw a furious Sister Flint enter the theatre, waving the now familiar instrument above her head. "Who is responsible for this?" she bellowed. "Boiling a valuable instrument, a Bronchoscope, complete with bulb and batteries - criminal!" There came a stunned silence! Before I could speak, a mouse like voice from the far end of theatre, said. "It was me. Sister." Then pointing at me as a witness in court fronts the accused, "he told me to do it!" "In my office, - Now," said Flint, a face like thunder. Standing in front of her desk I flinched at the tirade that followed. "Have you any idea how much these instruments cost and how we cope without them?" she fumed. "But what I find most despicable, you hadn't the guts to own up. I feel I have no option but to send you to Matron!" "Now hang on a moment Sister, don't be hasty," said a familiar voice. I gasped as no other than Charles Parker Nobbs came into the office. "I remember a Junior Sister, name escapes me, who once made a mistake, luckily this was sorted out before real harm was done, now what was her name?" "I'm sure it will come to me." "Out," said Sister Flint, I needed no second bidding. Was it my imagination or did the irascible Surgeon give me a wink as I passed through the door? My regard for Mr Charles Parker Nobbs changed immediately. I spent some four months in theatre, losing a stone in weight in the process. On reflection it is my candid belief that theatre staff are born, not made. I am the first to admit I would never make a theatre nurse, being too clumsy, awkward and sensitive and must have been a source of some irritation. Surgeons and theatre staff work under tremendous pressure and carry a heavy responsibility, is it any wonder that tempers fray.

My particular ordeal came to an end when I was eventually moved onto a Paediatric Ward which I thoroughly enjoyed and soon became pre-occupied with giving feeds and changing nappies. Theatre was now a thing of the past and far behind me.

CHAPTER ELEVEN
Cupid's Arrow and Matron's Enema

Life on the Children's Ward passed swiftly and smoothly enough. The Sister in charge of the unit, whose name was Savage who unlike her name, was both young and liberated and treated me no differently than my female colleagues. I became a dab hand at changing nappies and bottle-feeding babies. I couldn't help but think what my mates would say if they could see me in a gown, with a babe in my arms, testing the milk on the inside of my forearm before giving the feed.

"You'll make someone a damn good wife one day,"

said Sister Savage, with a laugh, as I walked around the cubicle, a baby's head wobbling into my neck, as I attempted to coax out a burp. Her good-natured remark made me smile and I could see the humour in it well enough. However, her face now took on a more serious look as I placed one gurgling and contented infant back in its cot.

"Mike, I want you to go with a suspected polio case to the Isolation Hospital in Sheffield," she said. "David is an eight-year-old boy who came in last night with a severe headache, neck stiffness, pyrexia and rigors. At first, meningitis was suspected, but he has since developed breathing and swallowing problems and will need to be on continuous oxygen and suction *en route*. I would normally ask Staff Nurse Burns to go, but as she is pregnant, I don't want to subject her to the risk. Do you think you can handle this?"

I quickly nodded my response. Some thirty minutes later saw me attired in a gown and mask in the back of the ambulance with my young charge. The lad certainly looked extremely poorly and was having difficulty in breathing, despite the continuous oxygen I was giving him.

"Want me to get a move on?" said the driver, seeing my worried expression.

"Yes, put your foot down," I replied, noting with concern the blue tinge spreading from the boy's lips to the lobes of both ears. I knew this was called cyanosis, a serious condition denoting lack of oxygen to the tissues. I felt the ambulance surge forward and gather momentum.

When I looked through the darkened glass, I saw houses flashing by and heard the shrill sound of the emergency bell clearing a way through the early morning traffic. In other circumstances, I would have found this experience both exciting and exhilarating, but I was far too worried to enjoy any part of it now. Swaying about in the speeding vehicle, I attempted to alternate the oxygen flow with suction, inserting a fine catheter down the throat to clear secretions, before replacing the breathing mask. Neither of these procedures appeared to make any difference to the blue tinge or the laboured breathing.

"We'll not be long now, David," I said, with a conviction I didn't really feel. The boy looked up at me, fair-haired and blue-eyed.

"I want me Mum," he gasped. "Get me Mum, Mister."

I was no substitute. I could only thank God his parents were being spared the ordeal of this moment. I knew, from the hurried briefing given by Sister Savage, that poliomyelitis was a disease caused by a virus which attacked the spinal cord, that children were most commonly affected - it used to be called infantile paralysis - and that the disease could be spread by droplet infection (airborne), or from faeces (ingested). In severe cases paralysis could occur. Commonly, the legs, intercostal muscles or diaphragm were affected. I knew that in David's case, the intercostal muscles that allow the chest wall, or ribs, to rise and fall were most likely affected. He also had swallowing problems, and was in danger of choking because he was unable to get rid of his saliva. Although vaccination was now available, usually given on a sugar lump, it was suspected that David had either slipped through the net, or his parents had refused the vaccine.

This hypothesising was all well and good, but no help in the present emergency situation. That journey was a nightmare. At one point, David appeared to stop breathing altogether. Thankfully, a combination of vigorous suction and oxygen saved the day.

Lodge Moor Hospital was situated in the green belt area of Sheffield, hence the protracted journey. I breathed a sigh of relief as the ambulance turned into the main drive, dominated by an enormous clock tower which looked oddly out of place. From what I could see of it, the wards were well spread out, all of single-storey design and inter-linked by lengthy corridors.

The few minutes spent at reception were an eternity to me, as I attempted to comfort my young charge, while still administering suction - an impossible task.

"Central One Ward," yelled the driver, quickly climbing back into the cab. They were, I was thankful to see, expecting us. Two white-coated doctors assisted us with the stretcher. After asking a few pertinent questions, they snatched the case notes from my hand and made a speedy dash for the ward entrance.

I leant against the back of the ambulance. Suddenly, I felt drained, exhausted almost, but what a feeling of relief. We had made it; David was in skilled hands at last.

"You look as though you could do with a cup of tea. Could you?"

I looked up and saw a pleasant-faced student nurse smiling down at me.

"I sure could," I said, following her into the ward kitchen. The ward appeared modern, spacious and airy, in complete contrast to the Victoria Royal, with its grim stone walls and dark interior.

"I'm Nurse Lingard - Judy, if you like - and you are?" Still smiling, she paused slightly, before handing me a mug of tea.

"Oh, just call me Mike," I said, with a laugh, sliding onto the large kitchen table. Now more relaxed, I swung my legs a little, before taking a swig of tea which was sweet and hot. Observing my colleague a little more closely now, my heart gave a skip. She was by far the prettiest nurse I had ever seen. Her eyes were of the deepest blue, set in a petite face, the mouth, nose, cheekbones, all delicate, all in perfect alignment. The hair, thick, long and luscious, was obviously taken up before being crammed beneath her cap, to conform to regulation neatness. But it was her inner personality that really bowled me over. I knew instinctively, when she spoke, that she was the one for me.

"It's rude to stare," she said, teasingly, laughter in her eyes. Blushing, I felt uncomfortably awkward and stupid. My pulse raced, while my mouth suddenly felt dry, in spite of the tea. In an effort to retrieve some semblance of dignity and normality, I asked about the unit.

"I'll show you round, if you like," she said, taking my cup from me as I slid quickly off the table. I followed her out into the ward and was reminded of the song 'Poetry in Motion'. What a figure she had!

"We have only two patients at present - sorry, three now, with young David," she corrected. I was conscious now of a rhythmic 'hiss' which emanated from two metal, oblong boxes, resembling giant incubators. On the side of these, two drum-shaped bellows rose and fell with monotonous regularity.

"Yes, Iron Lungs," whispered Nurse Lingard. "Come and meet Harry and Sandra, the occupants."

A head protruded through the top end of the box, above which was fixed an angled mirror. It became obvious that Harry viewed the world through reflected imagery: faces, books, TV, were all viewed through this narrow perspective. Far from being depressed, both occupants chatted with me cheerfully enough. In turn, I could detect no sense of bitterness from either. Feeling humbled, I asked how long they had been in the Lungs.

"Harry, eight years, Sandra, six. I'm Sister Faveretto, Sister in charge of the unit," a new voice interjected. A hand was outstretched. I took the proffered hand in surprise, being used to a more formal reception by Sisters. With her olive skin and dark hair, I guessed her to be Italian. She was certainly friendly.

"The Iron Lung works on positive and negative

pressure," she explained. "Harry and Sandra both have paralysed diaphragms and intercostal muscles. The machine pulls and pushes the chest wall in and out, thus allowing them to breathe. They can come out of the Lung, but only for an hour. While out, they have been taught to gulp or swallow air into the lungs, but can only keep this up for a limited period. You've done well with young David, by the way. He is already on a respirator."

"Thanks," I said, blushing once more, not used to praise, especially from a Sister. I turned to Nurse Lingard. "Are you training for your SRN, like me?" I asked.

"No," she replied, "RFN, Registered Fever Nurse. Actually, mine is the last group to train in this speciality before they close the register."

Sister Faveretto cut in once more. "With the advent of vaccination and immunisation, infectious diseases have been practically wiped out. This hospital has seen small pox, diphtheria epidemics, typhoid, scarlet fever, measles, whooping cough, TB - all practically non-existent now, thank goodness. We have, however, one of the finest Spinal Injury Units in the country, which has helped pioneer the treatment and care of paraplegics," she said with a smile.

"You coming, mate, or are you walking back?" The ambulance driver, obviously waiting impatiently for some time now, was eager to be off.

"Right," I said, "I'm coming." I said goodbye to Sister Faveretto, then turned to Nurse Lingard and bade her a stuttering farewell. It was now or never, as faint heart never won fair lady.

"I don't suppose I could see you again?" I asked.

"I don't think so," she replied. She pulled a chain from around her neck. From this dangled a huge engagement ring. I beat a hasty retreat, wishing the ground to open up beneath my feet.

"Better luck next time," said my ambulance driver colleague, with a grin. "I could have tipped you the wink; she's due to marry one of the consultants any time now!"

Over the next few weeks, Nurse Lingard became a distant memory; my mind was again occupied with the passing of exams. I could hardly believe that two years were practically up and it was time to sit The Preliminary State Examination Part 2. As usual, this was preceded by a six-week study block at The School of Nursing. Miss Grayson, our Tutor, did her best to instil confidence into the now-depleted group (five having packed in during the past year). In a futile attempt to clear her blocked sinuses, she gave the now-familiar snort.

"As you know," she said, "you are shortly due to sit your Preliminary State Examination. This will cover not only the principals and practice of nursing, but bacteriology and principles of asepsis, and first aid. You have completed several mock exams to prepare you for this, so you should be well acquainted with the subject matter and the system by now. However," she paused, as though to let the word 'this' sink in, "*this* time the examination is in two parts. You will have to contend with a written and a practical. I am allowed to tell you that the written part of the exam you will sit here, but the practical will be held at The Royal Hospital, Sheffield. There will be two Matrons in attendance, who will examine and question you for twenty minutes. Any questions?"

A few hands were raised, reminiscent of school kids asking permission to leave the room.

"Yes, nurse!"

Sonya stood up, blushing slightly, all eyes now focused on her.

"Do both Matrons question us at the same time, Miss Grayson?"

"Of course not," came the snorting reply. "You will

change over after twenty minutes and go to the other examiner, there being only two of you allowed in the room at any one time!"

"Bloody hell," whispered Sonya in my ear, "double trouble, double time!"

I nodded grimly in agreement.

"You are now about to enter your final year," Miss Grayson went on, "and will be obtaining a degree of specialist experience during this time. It is obligatory for you female nurses to undergo Obstetric and Gynaecology training and you will be seconded to our Sister hospital to enable you to undertake this. The male among us, however, will undertake a course of psychiatric nursing at Middlewood Hospital, Sheffield. All of you will do six weeks of community nursing, also. So, as you will gather, your final year will be both varied and interesting. This afternoon I shall be showing the film, To Jane a Son, as this shows a live birth scene and is quite graphic, the male amongst us will be excluded. You will read up a Venereal Diseases in the room next door Nurse Bolger." Miss Grayson paused briefly, beamed round the room, extricated herself, with some difficulty, from her tall chair, and slid down to earth with a bump.

There was the usual hubbub on her departure and, with moans and groans about placements and the forthcoming examinations, the group eventually broke up.

******

I stared down once more at the same yellow-coloured exam sheet, noted once again that no marks would be given for irrelevant matter, and that 'Candidates Must Attempt Four Questions *and not more than four*.' There were a total of seven questions on the paper, thus giving a choice of three to play with. I decided to start with: 'What can the nurse and other members of staff do to ensure that the patients get sufficient rest?' I then tackled the next three, which involved: 'Relieving a Mrs Brown of her constipation'; 'The collection of (a) Sputum (b) Faeces (c) Clean specimen of urine'; and 'Passengers injured in a bus crash. How would you approach the situation? Give reasons for your actions.'

In all, I felt I hadn't done too badly, and the rest of the group were all fairly optimistic, but we were less so after the practical.

The Royal Hospital was situated smack in the centre of the city. It was a large building, attached to a pillared, mausoleum-type structure, which had previously been a chapel of some sort and now served as an outpatients' department. A disgruntled porter directed us to the rear of the building, where we soon spied a board on which was a large arrow, beneath which was written: GNC Practical Examinations.

Wearing immaculate uniforms, starched caps and aprons, black stockings and shining shoes, the girls looked every inch professional nurses. I, on the other hand, had persuaded Mrs Pottle to give my jacket and trousers a special iron, and had spent a good half an hour polishing my shoes. All of us were wearing our obligatory personal exam numbers, and we sat waiting in nervous anticipation.

"What time is it?" somebody asked.

"Five to ten," came the reply.

This must be what it's like to be on death row, I thought, as a sudden feeling of foreboding hit my stomach. All heads turned as the door leading from the small annex suddenly opened and in stepped a Matron Examiner. She wore a uniform of grey, with a collar of intricate lace which matched her cap. Peering at us over half-moon spectacles which gave her face a magisterial look, she glanced down at the clipboard in her hand.

"Please respond to your number when called," she said, and proceeded to shout out the names on the list in front of her. Satisfied that all were present, she then gave a few detailed instructions.

"You will all be given a card bearing the time of your exam. Please be back here five minutes before the stated time. You will, before the start of the exam, be given ten minutes to familiarise yourselves with the room and its equipment.

"You will notice a volunteer patient in one of the beds. Please treat him with the utmost courtesy, should you be required to involve him in any nursing procedure. You will spend twenty minutes each with my colleague and me, and a bell will ring to inform you when it is time to change. You should then introduce yourself to the new examiner as quickly as possible. Once you have completed your exam, you should not converse with any colleague, but leave the hospital immediately. Any questions?"

There being none, she hastily distributed the time-cards to the group, then promptly disappeared. I glanced down at my card. Below my exam number was written, '12md', which meant that I had all of two hours to wait. There was the usual babble of conversation as we each discovered who was our partner in time. I had Mary Platts, so off we went with some of the others in search of a much-needed cup of coffee.

We sat in the dining room and watched our colleagues leave in pairs, until it was our time.

"Come on, Mary. Time to go," I said, with a cheerfulness I didn't feel.

"God, I hope I don't cop for dilution of lotions," she said, with a grimace.

I knew this was unpopular because it required the use of mathematics to work out various concentrations of lotions.

We entered the examination room at twelve on the dot

and were reminded about the ten-minute look-around time. As I gazed around the large room, I observed piles of sheets and blankets, trolleys, bowls, gallipots, lengths of tubing, syringes, instruments and a whole host of varied equipment. In a bed at the far end of the room sat our patient, a cheerful-looking man, with plastered-down hair and red-striped pyjamas. He was obviously thoroughly enjoying himself. I sure as hell wasn't. This was madness, surely, I thought. How on earth could you attempt to memorise all this in so short a time? Suddenly, a bell rang, and I saw one of the Matrons beckoning me. She was younger than her colleague, attired in a plum-coloured uniform, and her hair was parted in the middle, which made me think of Florence Nightingale.

First, she checked my number against the one on her clipboard, above which was fixed a large pocket-watch. Next, she gave her first set of instructions.

"Male nurse, would you set up a trolley for a lumber puncture," she said, pleasantly enough. Abject panic struck! I darted up and down the room, gathering the various bits of equipment I needed for my trolley. While doing so, I was thinking furiously about the reasons for the procedure. Think! Think! Think! I told myself I knew, vaguely, that a lumbar puncture involved inserting a needle between the lumbar vertebrae and into the spinal column to tap, or drain off, the fluid, but had never seen one done.

At last, all was gathered in and I stood in front of Florence Nightingale as she silently inspected my trolley, pausing occasionally to jot something down on her sheet. The dreaded questions followed.

"In what circumstances would you expect a lumbar puncture to be performed, nurse?"

She then stepped back, smiling at me expectantly, waiting for my answer. I thought back to my young polio victim.

"It is mainly used as a diagnostic procedure, Matron," I replied, fingers crossed.

"Yes, carry on, give examples," she stated, now staring at me intently.

"In poliomyelitis cases, it is used to detect any increase in white cells in the cerebrospinal fluid."

"Why should there be an increase in white cells?" she asked.

"Because, in the body's attempt to combat infection, white cells are often increased," I guessed.

"What other reasons for lumbar puncture can you give me?"

I racked my brains. "Meningitis?"

"Yes, and what are the signs and symptoms of meningitis?" I was now really sweating.

"Pyrexia, headache, stiff neck, rigors," I paused a while, looking at her, my mind a blank.

"Yes. Any other reasons?"

"To relieve pressure on the brain?"

"Can you name the instrument used to measure this pressure, nurse?"

I could not! Silence. The examiner scribbled a few comments on the sheet in front of her. I was now realising, that as I answered one question, this simply led to another. So, that was the technique they were using!

"Would you now quickly set up for the insertion of a naso gastric tube." A few minutes later saw me, tray in hand, standing in front of the younger matron. Good old milk drips. At least nurse Cobbin had taught me something! Swiftly she checked the contents of the tray but as she opened her mouth to probe further the shrill sound of the bell cut short any further questions, but not my ordeal, as this was simply the signal to change examiners.

I passed a flustered-looking Mary Platts *en route*. She

129

raised her eyes to heaven and whispered, "Absolute Cow!"

I now faced the Magistrate in grey, who once again peered at me over the top of her half-moon spectacles. She barked a question at me.

"How would you cope with a patient who was having an epileptic fit?"

"I would first of all ensure that the airway was kept clear, Matron," I answered.

"How would you do that?"

"I would place the patient on his side and ensure that the tongue was kept well forward."

"Demonstrate this for me," she said, and moved down the room in the direction of our volunteer patient. I dutifully followed. "Well, get on with it, nurse," she snapped, "we have not got all day."

The volunteer looked at me sympathetically, as I gently turned him onto his side and inserted two fingers under his jaw-line.

"Yes. What else could you use?"

"An airway, Matron."

"Get one!"

I sped about the room, in a frantic attempt to find an airway. Conscious that precious minutes were ticking away, I returned empty-handed. Horrors! She said nothing, but scribbled away furiously.

"Well, what else could you use?"

"A padded spoon, Matron?"

"Yes, yes, for what reason?"

"To prevent the patient biting his tongue."

"What precautions would you take when bathing an epileptic patient?"

"They should never be left alone, Matron, or, at least, kept under close, unobtrusive observation."

This answer was received with a curt nod and more scribbling on the pad.

"Now, set up a trolley in preparation for an *enema saponis*," she snapped, using the Latin term for soap-and-water enema. I sped off once more, in a desperate attempt to locate the elusive equipment required for the procedure. Breathless but triumphant, I returned with my trolley, complete with funnel, rectal catheter, rubber tubing, a large jug, bottle of green liquid soap, lotion thermometer, bedpan and bucket, draw sheet and rubber protector.

My mind flashed back to a crude little ditty I once heard at a hospital pantomime, which always made me smile. It was sung to the tune of 'Come Back to Sorrento' and went something like this:

Just a little enemata
With a jug of soap and water
We will cure your constipation
While you lie in meditation

Just slip the bedpan under,
Flatus sounds like thunder.
Good result, I shouldn't wonder,
By the smell that's hovering round.

"Well, what are you grinning at?" The examiner was glaring at me, her clipboard pressed tightly to her ample bosom.

"Nothing, Matron," I stammered. "Nerves, I suppose."

She gave me a long, hard, suspicious look, before delivering what was to be her final question.

"What are the signs and symptoms of faecal impaction?"

"There will be a history of constipation Matron," I blurted. "What if your patient is suffering from senile dementia and unable to give such a history," she snapped.

"The patient may well present with diarrhoea," I

131

replied. "Why?" came the immediate response.

"Because peristaltic action that moves the faeces along the bowel may increase below the impaction causing the loose stools," I replied. There now came a pause as she scribbled furiously on the clipboard in front on her desk.

"Now how would you prepare your patient for his emema?"

Saved by the bell! My answer was cut short. I was reprieved!

"You may go," said my inquisitor, her head still down, as she continued to mark off the contents of my trolley.

Once outside, I met up with Mary. "How did you get on?" we said, in unison. We laughed, because we both replied, "Failed."

******

Later on, in The Grapes, never had a pint tasted so good! I had decided to treat myself and drank in comfortable solitude. Completely relaxed now, I allowed my mind to wander away from hospitals and exam rooms, but found my thoughts once again centred on Nurse Judy Lingard. Since that first meeting, I had thought of her constantly, in spite of trying to wipe her image from my mind but her face was becoming more and more difficult to visualise. Someone slipped a coin into the Juke Box and pushed the select button. "Dum, Dum, Dum, Dummy, Doah" – came the opening words of Roy Orberson's 'Only the Lonely' appearing to mock me further.

The words of advice from that ambulance driver, 'Better luck next time', kept repeating themselves with irritating regularity, only adding to my torment of unrequited love. In a final effort to banish such thoughts from my mind, I returned once more to the happenings of the day. Had I passed? In my present mood, I cared little. I picked up my empty glass, approached the bar and ordered a refill. Well, it was all in the lap of the Gods once more, I mused, or was it all dependent on 'Just A Little Enemata?' Perhaps!

CHAPTER TWELVE
You Don't have to be, but if you are it helps!

Abandon hope, all you that enter here, I thought, looking up at the huge arched entrance, above which, etched in a scroll of stone, were the words: South Yorkshire Asylum 1878.

The turreted buildings, standing in acres of grounds, were

of similar design to the Victorian prisons still in use today and certainly looked as grim and cheerless. I had, much to my amazement, successfully passed my preliminary exams and been posted to this large mental hospital for a spot of psychiatric experience. It was with a mixture of excitement and dread that I presented myself at six a.m. on this dark, wet morning to the Charge Nurse of Ward 36. Following the signs, I made my way down endless corridors. When, at last, I reached my destination, I found the ward was in total darkness. Light was coming from under the door of what I took to be an office; I knocked and walked in. There were four people in the office, drinking tea. They all turned round and looked at me suspiciously as I announced my name and said whence I came.

"Grab a mug of tea, lad, and sit thi sen down," said the eldest of the group. "I'm Paul Freeman, Charge Nurse of this 'ere lot."

The group quickly lost interest in me and started to talk between themselves again. I poured myself a mug of tea from a large pot and found a chair, before self-consciously glancing at my colleagues between swigs of tea. There were three males and one female. None wore uniform as such; however, one of the males stood out from the rest. He stared vacantly into space, his mug drooped from his hands, and occasionally tea slopped down his trousers. His hair was halfway down his back, and suspended from one of his lobes hung a large earring. Suddenly, the penny dropped: this was obviously a patient who had suffered a disturbed night, and been brought into the office by the staff so they could keep an eye on him. I observed him between half-closed lids. Definitely a psychopath. No, perhaps a schizophrenic?

"We don't wake 'em up till seven a.m., lad," said Mr Freeman, including me in the conversation once more.

"What about this chap?" I asked, nodding my head

towards the long-haired tea-slopper. "Had a bad night, has he?"

There was a pregnant pause before the room erupted with great guffaws of laughter.

"Bloody hell, he thinks you're a patient, Steve. Well, he's not far wrong, is he?" howled the Charge Nurse, wiping his streaming eyes with the back of his hand.

"Cheeky bastard! I'm a Staff Nurse. I might have known a general nurse would talk such crap," snapped my now-disgruntled colleague.

God, what a way to start a new shift, I thought, wishing the ground would open up and remove me swiftly from this predicament.

At seven a.m. on the dot, the three staff got to their feet and made for the ward, leaving me with Mr Freeman. He pulled the bottom drawer from his desk and placed his feet on it, before tilting his chair to an angle of forty-five degrees. Then, removing a pipe from his top pocket, he proceeded, with the aid of a large number of matches, to light it. At last, it burst into life, billowing great clouds of smoke and ash into the air. For a while he disappeared from view into a dense fog which eventually cleared and I was able to see his features once more. He was, I guessed, of middle age. He had a stocky build and a thick thatch of jet-black hair, starting to grey at the temples. Obviously Yorkshire born and bred and proud of it, he was a typically 'no nonsense' kind of a bloke and I liked him.

"Aye, you'll like it on 'ere, lad," he said. "We've some interesting cases at moment." He paused to inspect the pipe in his hand before continuing. "I'll give thee a bit of pocket-book psychiatry that will stand thee in good stead: thy first lesson, if tha likes. There are two types of patients in this hospital: those suffering from neurosis and those suffering with psychosis. In plain man's language, the first group usually know they are ill and want to get better, while the latter group most times don't know they are ill, and can't know."

"What about the first group?" I asked, fascinated. "What kind of conditions are they suffering from?"

Between pipe-puffs, he filled me in. "Those with depression, anxiety states, phobias, compulsive behaviour; they all fall into that category. You will find out more about these patients when you leave this Ward for a spell on the Day Centre. People with the more serious mental states, such as schizophrenia and psychopathy, would fall into the latter group. Some schizophrenics are also paranoid; they think people are plotting against them. They may think their food is poisoned and suchlike, or that they are being spied upon by hidden cameras."

"I see," I said, beginning to realise what an awful thing mental illness really was. I was about to ask what a psychopath was, when Mr Freeman suddenly snatched the pipe from his mouth, lowered his chair and rose to his feet.

"Steve," he bellowed, "get yourself in 'ere, pronto!"

Staff Nurse Steve appeared at the door, still looking sullen, no doubt as a result of my previous insult.

"Now, Steve, no grudges. Lad didn't intend no harm. Come on, shake on it." Steve proffered a reluctant hand, which I clasped firmly.

"Sorry, mate, no insult intended," I said, and was relieved to see his face break out into a grin.

"And none taken," he replied. "Come on, I'll show you round," he added, cheerfully enough.

The ward consisted of thirty-two beds. Two wards were of the seclusion type. These were single rooms; their doors had a round window and handles on the outside only. A peep inside gave an austere view of a single mattress at floor level and little else.

"We only use these for violent incidents, which are rare, actually, contrary to popular belief," said Steve, with a grin. "Come on, we'll head for the day room. Breakfasts have been given out."

When we entered the communal sitting room, I was confronted by a bewildering array of patients. Some sat staring vacantly into space, while others agitatedly paced up and down the room.

"A mixed bag," explained Steve, indicating for me to sit down. "Unlike general nursing, most of our work is devoted to observation. You will notice that, when we give our reports at the end of each shift. For instance, we may notice that a certain patient has become more withdrawn, which is an indication of a deepening of his depression, or perhaps a patient may inform you that he intends to end it all."

"If they talk about it, they don't usually do it, is that right?" I suggested.

"The opposite, actually," replied Steve. "If they talk about it, then it's in their mind to do it!"

I began to realise what a skilful psychiatric nurse Steve was, in spite of his laid-back appearance, and cursed myself for my stupid initial mistake. The other two staff now joined us in our debate and seemed friendly enough. Joy was a tall, thin, black girl with spectacles, who introduced herself as a second-year psychiatric nurse. Her colleague, on the other hand, was a plump, stocky lad by the name of Bob, who was a nursing auxiliary. I was just about to ask Joy how she found work on the ward, when Paul Freeman popped his head round the door.

"Job for the new man," he said. "Pop over to Ward 18, will you, and convey fifteen patients to the dentist. They're short-staffed and can't spare anyone."

"Ward 18 is long-stay. The patients are very institutionalised and do exactly what you tell them. You shouldn't have any bother," whispered Steve.

After travelling down a myriad of corridors, I arrived at Ward 18, where I found my patients already waiting.

They stood in single file, some apprehensively wringing their hands, some with trousers halfway up their shins. They looked at me with vacant, expressionless eyes. A plump woman in a blue Sister's uniform approached.

"All for the dentist. Routine check-up. Know where it is?" She looked at me suspiciously.

I knew the dentist's room was next to reception, so I nodded, eager to impress.

"Right," she said, with a clap of her hands, "off you go then."

Like a set of startled horses, the patients left the ward at breakneck speed. I had a difficult job to keep up with them.

"Slow down!" I yelled. But they paid no heed. Suddenly the corridor forked. I watched, horrified, as half my patients went one way and half the other. Out of the corner of my eye, I saw two slip through into another ward.

"Stop," I yelled, to no avail. Following the row of now-depleted patients, I could only watch in helpless dismay as, one by one, they disappeared from view. I arrived breathlessly at the dentist and asked if they had turned up. A shake of the head brought home my worst fears. Panic gripped me; my first day in a mental hospital and fifteen patients had escaped! I searched the grounds for a good hour, and then checked back with the dentist. Still, he shook his head. With heavy tread, I made my way back to Ward 18, imagining the press headlines: FIFTEEN MENTAL PATIENTS ESCAPE CUSTODY - STUDENT NURSE TO BLAME.

The ward Sister looked up at me when I walked in.

"I've lost fifteen patients, Sister," I said, with a sense of impending dread.

139

"Yes," she said, "I know. They all made their way back here. Are you a general student?"

I confirmed that this was so and watched, shamefaced, as she slowly shook her head.

******

I was three weeks into working on Ward 36, and getting accustomed to the various patients, when disaster struck. Breakfasts had been given out and I was sitting in the day ward, along with a group of patients, when I was confronted by a persistent and agitated young man.

"Let me show you this strangle hold; it won't take a minute," he said. I naturally declined his invitation. However, this made him even more agitated.

"Go on," he pleaded. "It won't take long."

"No," I replied. "Go away."

This only served to increase his agitation and

persistence. He now began to jump up and down in front of me, like a Red Indian doing a rain dance.

"Go on, go on, won't take a minute, let me show you!" he screeched.

I sized him up; he was of stocky build, but much shorter than I, which gave me added confidence. What was it they said? Humour them, that was it. I would do just that and calm the situation down. I rose to my feet and noted, with satisfaction, his small stature.

"Right," I said. "Show me."

He placed both hands round my throat. With arms outstretched, he stared at me through slate-grey, expressionless eyes.

"Satisfied?" I said, moving to sit down once more. It was then that it happened! Suddenly, my legs were kicked from under me, sending me crashing to the floor. In a trice, he was on me. He was sitting on my chest, with both knees on my biceps. I was totally helpless. Slowly but deliberately, my captor placed a forearm against my throat and slowly increased the pressure. With his free hand, he groped for the carotid artery running down my neck. When he found it, he stabbed two stubby fingers hard into the flesh sending a searing pain deep into my left ear. As I stared up at the ceiling, I knew I was going to die. Very little air was reaching my lungs now, as I thrashed about in a desperate attempt to gain more oxygen. Slow strangulation is a terrible thing. My lungs screamed for air as my body grew weaker. Suddenly, there was a scuffle and it was all over. Willing hands pulled me to my feet. A patient had raised the alarm and staff had come running from several wards. I stood, hands on knees, taking in great gulps of air, while the patient was dragged off to seclusion, held between four staff.

******

"Tha's a daft bugger, what are you?"

"A daft bugger, Charge Nurse," I replied, suitably mortified. Seated in Mr Freeman's office, I was now suffering the after-effects of shock. I was conscious that my voice as well as my hands now shook.

"E're, get that down thee," he said, handing me a steaming mug of hot, sweet coffee. He lit up the now-familiar pipe and tilted back his chair to its usual angle. He looked at me, an amused expression in his eyes. "Well, lad, you certainly know how to pick 'em. Alan Renshaw is one of the most crafty and dangerous psychopaths in the hospital."

"How was I to know?" I asked, taking a sip of scalding-hot coffee.

"You weren't, lad. He slipped off his ward somehow and found you, an inexperienced nurse. It's my guess, he sussed that out. He is a clever beggar that one."

"What is a psychopath? I asked.

"Good question, lad," replied Mr Freeman, between pipe puffs. "The psychologists have been trying to work that one out for years. The cause is unknown, although it is thought that certain childhood influences can play a part in its make-up. They are of cold personality, usually manipulative and cunning; they bully the other patients and generally cause trouble, if not kept firmly in check. In other words, they are a pain in the arse on any ward. I could go on and on giving you loads of psychological jargon, but it would only confuse you. Do you feel up to finishing your shift, or do you want to go home?"

"I'm OK now," I said, taking a final swig of coffee. "I'll carry on."

"Good man," said Mr Freeman, from behind a cloud of blue smoke. "Off tha goes, then. Shut door, on thi way out."

******

I had heard of ECT (electro-convulsive therapy), but, of course, I had never seen it carried out. This was to change one day, when I was asked if I would like to view the procedure. I had got to know the patient who was to undergo the treatment and knew him to be very clinically depressed. The patient's name was John and his story a rather sad one. He had, at the age of forty-three, lost his wife to cancer, after having nursed her for several years. A self-employed printer, his business had suffered and he eventually went bust. With two children of school age to support and mounting debts, he had carried gamely on until, one morning, he decided he could no longer cope. His thoughts of suicide over the previous few months had, oddly, comforted him. It was a way out of his misery; he would be with his wife again. When he cut his throat with a Stanley knife, he made a complete hash of it. He missed the jugular and cut through the trachea, or wind-pipe, and lived. Now, in spite of antidepressant therapy, he lived a life of utter hopelessness and dread.

The anaesthetist explained the procedure to me as it was carried out. First, John was given intravenous Pentothal, which rendered him unconscious; he was then given a muscle relaxant, before being intubated, then bagged (respirated manually). From a small wooden box, two electrodes were attached to the patient's temples and the electric current turned on. Immediately the patient began to fit. The convulsions gradually subsided within about half a minute.

"That's about it," said the anaesthetist. "All that remains is to get him recovered and allow him to recuperate a while."

"Are there any side effects?" I asked.

"Not really," he replied. "He may have a bit of a

143

headache for a while, which will pass off."

"Is this a one off?" I enquired.

"No, this chap's due for five more," replied the anaesthetist, glancing at his notes, "and don't ask me how it jolts people out of depression, because I don't know!"

Over the next few weeks, I saw a dramatic change in John; he was a totally different person, bright-eyed, alert, cheerful and looking forward to going home. He had truly been given a new lease of life.

Seated in Mr Freeman's office on my final day, I felt sadness at leaving the relaxed and informal atmosphere of his ward.

"Well, lad, how's tha found it? I told thee it were interesting, didn't I?"

I nodded in affirmation of his remark. "Yes," I said, "I've learnt a lot and I thank you." And I meant it. Mr Freeman adopted his usual forty-five degree stance and clasped both hands at the back of his neck.

"Aye, lad, it were a different job in my day; very few drugs, padded cells, brute force - this place was a hell-hole in them days. But things have changed for the better, and quite rightly so. Don't waste your time in general nursing, lad. You've the makings of a first-class mental nurse. Come back and do your training."

This was praise indeed! I clasped his hand and thanked him once more. I had reached the door when he shouted my name. I turned round.

"Mike, do you know what a psychopath is?"

"Yes, I rather think I do and always will," I said as, laughing, I left his ward.

******

The day centre turned out to be a fine-looking house, previously owned by a wealthy steel magnate and bequeathed many years ago to a charitable trust. It stood in its own grounds and gave one the feeling of complete eloquence. It was with such a feeling that I presented myself to a Sister Fairburn the nurse in charge of the unit, who had her office on the first floor of this grandiose building. She was both pleasant and young and I immediately gained the impression that we would get along just fine. Seated in the oak-panelled office, whose long-shuttered windows gave an impressive view of sweeping lawns, I relaxed a little, waiting expectantly for an introduction.

Clearing her throat, she smiled, proffered her hand, then said by way of introduction, "Jane. You, I take it, are Mike?" Not waiting for a reply she quickly came to the point. "As you well know, this is a day unit for the treatment of neurotic disorders. We are only a small staff consisting of Dr Lewis, psychiatrist, myself, Sister in charge, Ann, a Nurse Therapist, and Susan, our Staff Nurse. You'll have the opportunity of meeting them later. The patients arrive at nine a.m. and leave at four p.m. Their span of treatment varies with the condition and type of progress made. Any questions so far?"

"Yes," I said, "what kind of problems do your patients suffer from?"

She smiled. "Many and varied," came the reply. She then went on to explain, "Most of our patients are suffering from manifestations of the anxiety state, namely, phobias. These phobias are diverse and, if left untreated, can severely restrict the patient's lifestyle, resulting in a kind of living hell. You will no doubt have heard of agoraphobia - fear of open spaces. We have several patients suffering from this condition." She gave a sudden smile. "They say the worst attended yearly event is the Agoraphobic Club's annual dinner." A sense of humour, I thought; I liked that. "I don't intend to make light of

145

phobic states." Her face now took on a more serious look. "They really do cause our patients a lot of grief, as you will no doubt discover."

"What other types of condition do you treat here?" I asked.

"Compulsive disorders, another distressing complaint," she replied. "These can take the form of repetitive actions that torment the patient, forcing him eventually to comply. For example, have you never felt the need to check the back door or gas taps before or after leaving your house? Have you ever had to turn back to make double sure?"

I nodded. I could see where she was coming from, having experienced a little sample of this when on my last placement. Ralph, one of the elderly patients on the unit, used to recite a repetitive little ditty, that went something like this:

It is easy to be happy when life flows along like a song
But the man who's worthwhile
Is the man who can smile
When everything goes dead wrong!

As soon as he had finished, off he went again, then again and again, until after a shift of eight hours, on getting home, you discovered you had been brainwashed into saying the damn ditty in your head whether you wanted to or not!

Jane went on. "Well, imagine that feeling magnified a hundred times and that no matter how many times you check and re-check, you feel the compulsion to return and check again. To illustrate this, we once had a driving instructor as a patient here who was tormented by the idea that a child may have crawled under his back wheels! Every morning, before reversing from his drive onto the road, he was forced to check and check again! Each time he entered his car, he had this fear that between the time of checking and getting back into the car, a child may have had time to crawl under the wheels. It took between fifteen and twenty checks each day before, drained and exhausted, he felt able to pull out onto the road."

"How would you treat such a condition?" I asked, fascinated.

"With behavioural therapy, patience and a great deal of hard work," she said, with the now-familiar smile. "Really, a lot of this work entails getting the patients to face up to their fears and anxieties. Once they begin to understand how these things come about, they start to lose the fear and begin to improve." I nodded my head slowly, beginning to see what a complex mechanism the human brain really was. "Right, lecture over. Are you feeling fit?" she said, getting to her feet. "It's downstairs for you, my lad. Let's introduce you to the team."

The team, I was relieved to discover, were just as friendly as Jane. What a change from the formality of the general hospital – Sister, on first name terms. I could hardly believe it! Dr Lewis looked every inch the psychiatrist; aged about forty with a goatee beard and tiny round-framed glasses, he gave a friendly nod. Ann, the Nurse Therapist, was pleasant enough; tall and slim, she appeared a bit of a recluse. Susan, by way of contrast, was stout and very outgoing. She shook my hand, and I immediately warmed to her.

"I'll leave you in Susan's capable hands now," said Jane. "Must be off, lots to catch up on." With this, she shot passed me and disappeared upstairs. Susan then took me on a whistle-stop tour of the house, which consisted of four large rooms downstairs, some with antique furniture, and toilets and kitchen.

"There are a further five rooms upstairs, mostly used as offices and for therapy," she explained.

147

Outside, the grounds were vast with several large greenhouses, sadly in a state of neglect. There were also several outbuildings, stables and the like.

"How they must have lived when this was in its prime," I commented with a sigh. "I could really fancy myself as lord of this manor."

Susan laughed. "It would take a bit more pay than you earn to keep this place going."

I had to agree.

"Come on, the patients will be arriving soon. I'll fill you in as we walk." Susan was a good teacher; although qualified less than three years, she certainly knew her stuff. "The patients arrive at nine. Some make their own way, while others that live further afield usually come by ambulance minibus. They all have their own treatment programmes worked out by Dr Lewis and Ann. It's our job to see these carried out and Jane has asked for you to take part in this with one particular patient of which I'll fill you in later."

"Blimey," I exclaimed, alarmed but flattered, hoping it wouldn't be too complicated.

On our return, we discovered the patients had arrived and were gathered together in the spacious front room. There were nine in number, consisting of six women and three men. Some chattered fifty to the dozen, while others remained aloof, staring vacantly into space. Susan soon got to work.

"Come on, exercise time, up on your feet," she cried, clapping her hands together. "George, turn the record player on please. You shouldn't have to be told, you've done it often enough." A rather miserable youth that I assumed was George, slowly made his way to a record player at the far end of the room and turned it on. To the sounds of 'Lying in the Arms of Mary', we all followed Susan, swaying from side to side, arms above heads. There followed a succession of other tunes, each accompanied by a variety of gyrations. Some of the patients entered into the spirit of the thing while others simply went through the motions.

"Time for a cuppa," shouted Susan, as a large trolley complete with steaming mugs came into view. "The patients take it in turns to do the trolley and washing up," she explained. "Grab a couple of mugs, Mike, I want a word with you in private." Mystified, I followed her into the adjoining room seating myself next to her at the large dinning table.

"You remember me telling you earlier, that Jane wanted you to get involved with one of the treatment programmes?" I nodded my head in agreement. "Well, I think I have just the patient for you. His name is Frank and he is an agoraphobic. He has a massive inferiority complex brought about by a combination of disastrous events in his life. He first of all lost his mother who was very close to him. He then discovered his wife was having an affair, after which, she subsequently left him. Shortly after this, he was demoted at work, due, we presume, to poor performance."

"What work does he do?" I enquired.

"He was a foreman in one of the larger steelworks. Now he's a labourer," Susan replied. She went on, "He has become very introverted and withdrawn, so you're going to have your work cut out to get him motivated. That's the easy bit. Now for the care plan. We want you to get him outdoors first, then onto a bus and eventually into the city centre. We want him to get used to his fear feelings so that over a period of time they become less threatening. It's what we call flooding. However, we have to start way back; we can't rush things, otherwise he would lose even more confidence."

I was beginning to understand. "So we start with small

149

improvements at first, hoping to build on these?" I said.

"That's right," said Susan. "Let me explain further. We have a lady in here with arachnophobia: fear of spiders. She is all but cured, but it's taken months. We first got her to sit at the far end of a room, away from a spider in a closed box. Gradually her panic attacks lessened as she got more used to this and she could then bear to have the box a little nearer to her. A glass lid was then introduced so that now she could actually see the spider. Eventually, she could bring herself to touch the box, and then actually sit with the box on her knee. We hope soon to get her to handle a spider. So you see, now, what a long process it is to bring about cure. Another lady called Muriel has a fear of thunder storms, believing she will be struck by lightning, so she never goes out, even on the sunniest day without a cloud in the sky. She fears she could run into one. In this case, we get her to sit in a darkened room, then simulate a thunder storm by the use of tapes and lighting effects."

"Is it working?" I enquired.

"To early to tell," came the reply. "Come on, let's introduce you to Frank."

We found Frank sitting with the other eight patients. He was a big chap, I would guess about 6 foot, 4 inches tall, weighing about 16 stone. He hardly looked the agoraphobic type; in fact, quite the opposite.

"Frank, this is Mike, who is going to help you," said Susan by way of introduction. Frank, partly raising himself out of his chair, clasped my hand in a very weak handshake.

"Right, I'm off," said Susan. "Come to the office when you've done chatting, Mike. See you later."

After she was gone, Frank and I stared at one another as I racked my brains for something to say, in an effort to put an end to this awkward silence.

"So you're Frank. I've heard a lot about you," I said,

with a lightness I didn't feel.

"Oh aye, and what's that then, all bad I suppose?" came the rather sullen reply.

"Not a bit," I replied with a laugh. "Why should you think that?"

"Because I'm a bloody failure, that's why. Just look at me, a bloke my size, afraid to go out!"

Even to my inexperienced eye I could detect a great deal of suppressed anger and bitterness both in tone and body language.

"You've been through a lot, Frank. I'm not here to judge you, but help you if I can," I said, with a confidence I didn't feel. Frank's response to this was to slump back in his chair with a sigh, a look of complete hopelessness adorning his features. Well, I was hardly making earth-shattering progress, so I tried another approach. "Look, Frank, you and I have got to work together on this. I know it's not going to be easy but I'm willing to give it my best. How about you?"

"I don't know, I don't really want to think about going out; it makes me feel panicky," came the reply. I had run out of ideas, it was obviously time to seek further advice.

"Tell you what, Frank," I said, "let's leave it there for the time being. I'll see you later."

Upstairs, I joined the gang of four, who appeared to be in conference.

"Come in, Mike," said Jane. "How did you get on with Frank?"

"Not very well, I'm afraid," I replied. "He doesn't appear to be particularly drawn to me."

"He won't be," replied Dr Lewis with a grin. "He sees you as a threat - you are the one making him face up to an unpleasant situation, a situation he wishes to avoid at all costs."

"On top of that, he has a very low self-esteem,"

interjected Ann, the Nurse Therapist. She went on, "Don't get discouraged, it's not you. He is the same with all the staff. This afternoon, get him to have a game of table tennis - he likes that. You can perhaps build on this to form a closer relationship. While we're on the subject, can I borrow Mike for a moment, Jane? This would be as good an opportunity as any to discuss Frank's treatment programme with him." Jane nodded her agreement as we moved off into the next office.

"I want you to start as soon as possible with this," said Ann, staring across at me from behind her desk, "tomorrow if at all possible. I will be seeing Frank this afternoon so will go over in some detail again what is expected of him. He knows the score, so don't let him fool you. Each morning I want you to take Frank down the drive. He will most likely throw a wobbler but I want you to persevere. I want you to cross the road and stand at the bus stop. Next week, each day, I want you and Frank on the bus, not to get off, but to return here from the terminus. The following and, dare we hope, final week, you and Frank will get off the bus at the terminus, walk down the road and back again. It's a busy shopping centre in the middle of town so it will be a real challenge. I will be telling Frank to use his fearometre to help him keep in control."

"What's a fearometre?" I asked intrigued.

"It's a scale of nought to ten that we get the patients to use in fear situations, ten being the highest fear reading and nought, the lowest. Its purpose is to give the patient some vestige of control over their fear; in other words, they can measure the degree of anxiety they feel at any particular moment. Frank calls it his Richter scale - you know, the scale used to measure earthquakes," she said with a grin. She went on, "One word of warning. Agoraphobic patients often suffer severe panic attacks, which cause great distress. They actually feel they are going to collapse or die."

"What do I do if faced with that situation?" I asked, not feeling at all confident myself.

"Simply keep calm; they never do die, it's all in the mind. You can usually reassure them and talk them through it," said Ann. "I know we appear to be asking a lot of you, but we're so short-staffed at present. Both Jane and Susan are running several programmes at the same time."

"Don't worry," I said with a confidence I didn't feel, "I am sure everything will go just fine!"

******

Over the next couple of weeks I got a lot closer to Frank, mostly due to the fact that he was good at table tennis and I wasn't. This actually helped to boost his flagging ego, which turned out to be no bad thing under the circumstances. It had, however, been no easy task, as each morning saw me accompanying Frank down the drive to the bus stop with the inevitable ensuing succession of panic attacks.

"What number now, Frank?" I would enquire of my gasping white-faced patient.

"Oh my God. Ten! Ten!" would come the rasping reply. Then a little later, "Eight, I think I'm eight."

"That's good, Frank," I would say, "very good. You see, your fear is getting less."

Exactly the same pattern emerged on the bus, which got us a few hard stares from fellow passengers, but I really felt we were making progress. Each day I had to update Ann on the progress made.

"It's now or never, Mike. Next week it's off the bus and a walk in town!"

The following Monday dawned grey and dull, with a hint of rain to come. This did little to allay the feelings of foreboding I had awoken with. These feelings were not improved, when, quite by accident, I observed Frank paying off a taxi driver at the bottom of the drive. He had the previous week convinced me that he was now making his own way into the unit by bus. Why should he tell such a blatant untruth to me, his helper and confidant?

Seated upstairs at the rear end of the bus, I relaxed a little, as Frank, now running at Richter scale seven, lit up a fag, appearing to be more at ease. However, the business with the taxi, for some reason, continued to irritate me as, following Frank's lead, I stared aimlessly out of the window. Another odd thing that struck me was that today, Frank was wearing not one, but three pairs of sunglasses. I could only assume, that either this gave him added confidence, or was an attempt to hide from his problem! However, on arrival at our destination I was cheered to discover that Frank's reading was five and that everything appeared to be going well.

"Come on, Frank, one more step for mankind," I said, likening our venture to the famous moonwalk, not dissimilar to my way of thinking. Frank needed no further prompting. To my amazement, pushing past me, he leapt down the stairs three at a time, onto the platform and on to the street.

Eventually catching up with him, I said, rather breathlessly, "Right, Frank, off we jolly well go, to the end of the shopping precinct and back."

Town was pretty crowded with early morning shoppers as we weaved in and out of the throng. All appeared to be going swimmingly and we were approaching the end of the group of shops when disaster struck. Frank went suddenly deathly pale and started clutching at his throat.

"I can't breath, I'm going to die," he gasped.

"No, you're not, Frank. Take some deep breaths, and try and relax," I said, in an effort to placate him. "What's your present reading?" I asked, trying to gain control.

"Gone off the bloody scale," came the rasping reply. Propping him up against a shop doorway, I attempted to loosen his collar and tie with one hand while supporting him with the other.

"I can't make it back, don't leave me," he said, suddenly locking his arm into mine. Any attempt to extricate myself was met with an increase in the vice-like grip - he was ruddy strong!

"Look, Frank," I said in desperation, "I promise not to leave you. It's more than my job's worth. Let's make it slowly back to the bus where you will start to feel better. Come on, let's go. You can still keep hold of my arm if you like," I pleaded. "What's your scale at the moment?"

"Eight," came the sullen reply.

"Well, there you are then," I replied. "You see, it's already on the decline."

I will never know if it was common sense talking, or deep breathing, or the Richter scale, or a combination of all three that saved the day. Suddenly Frank relaxed, appearing to come to his senses. Slowly, linking arms, we made it back to the bus. What an odd couple we must have looked as passers-by looked over their shoulders at us before scurrying past.

"Mike, that you?" said a familiar voice.

I turned and suddenly my mouth went dry. There she was, a second-year student from my old hospital.

"Muriel, how lovely to see you," I said with a sickly grin. "Can I introduce you to Frank? We're just out for the morning."

"So I gather," she said, a look of amusement on her face. "Come here often, do you?"

Seated once more on the bus, Frank turned to me, a satisfied smile on his face. "By the way, I'm six now," he said.

"That so, Frank?" I replied. "I'm ten!"

Back at the Day Centre, I reported the morning's disastrous events to the group, a combination of three weeks' work down the pan.

"You did your best, Mike. I blame myself really," said Ann. "I think in retrospect we probably pushed him too hard."

"You may be right," interjected Dr Lewis. "However, I think in light of this, there is more to our Frank than meets the eye. I wonder if his agoraphobia is masking something much more deep-seated. We will have to look into this more closely."

"Should he come off the programme then?" said Jane.

"Yes, I think that would be wise for now," replied Dr Lewis. "I will see him next week. Let's see how we go from there."

"By the way, Mike leaves us today," remarked Susan. "Have you learned anything from your stay with us?"

"Yes, I rather think I have," I replied. "The mind takes a long time to heal."

"You can say that again," they all replied with a laugh.

"Fancy a game of table tennis, Mike?" said Frank, later that afternoon. It was the first time he had called me by name. I felt a little sad - just as I was getting closer to him I was about to leave. As usual, I let him win.

CHAPTER THIRTEEN
Success, success, success!

My period of psychiatric experience was quickly followed by a stint of district nursing, which was spent with a Sister Davies, a plump, robust woman, who was the proud owner of a new Morris Minor motorcar. I found patients more rebellious in their own homes, far less in awe of us than their hospital counterparts.

"We are guests in their homes," Sister Davies explained, "and we always have to remember that fact."

Our days were taken up with giving early morning insulin injections, doing various varicose ulcer dressings, removing sutures and performing numerous bed baths. Most of our patients were elderly and infirm, which made for slow, methodical work. I had to admire the district nurses who worked alone, had few basic facilities and had, literally, to think on their feet most of the time.

During my period of training with Sister Davies, we called twice each day to a very affluent-looking house called Runcliffe Hall. Situated on the outskirts of the city, complete with winding gravel drive and covered in ivy, it was every inch the millionaire's mansion, which, in actual fact, was exactly what it was. Our patient, a thin emaciated old man, was doubly incontinent and totally bedfast. The work, extremely unpleasant, tedious and time-consuming, involved a complete bed bath to clean him up, the application of zinc and castor oil ointment to elbows, ankles and other vulnerable areas, and dressing a very nasty, gangrenous sacral pressure sore with a mixture of cod liver oil and Eusol. On lifting back the bedclothes, the

157

warm stench of the fish oil combined with the smell of necrosis and faeces is best left to the imagination. I really had to admire Sister Davies who had long tackled this onerous chore totally on her own with cheerfulness, compassion and dogged determination. Although our patient was suffering from, among other things, senile dementia, she chatted away to him fifty to the dozen asking if he was comfortable or feeling better, even though the response to her dialogue was always pure gibberish. The relatives of the old man (who, by all accounts, was worth a small fortune), were his sister and brother of whom we saw little, being usually escorted to and from the room by the Butler or Senior Parlour Maid.

Over the next few days, in spite of our ministrations, our patient appeared to deteriorate more and more. On arriving back at the clinic one day, we received an urgent call to return to the house where we discovered our patient had suddenly died. The sister, a small, willowy woman with beady eyes, looked at us disapprovingly.

"He's in a bit of a state and the doctor's due to arrive at any minute," she said, hovering a safe distance from the bedroom door. It was obvious why we had been sent for - the deceased, before departing this life, had covered himself and most of his surroundings with his bodily functions. Undaunted, we carried out last offices, leaving one spotless corpse complete with clean white sheets both above and below. After our efforts, we were duly escorted from the house with the usual decorum, the doors closing softly behind us.

It came as some surprise when, a fortnight later, a request arrived for Sister Davies to attend Runcliffe Hall to pick up a little something.

"Perhaps he's left you something in his will," I said.

"Don't be daft," came the reply, but I could see she was as intrigued as I was.

On our arrival the following day, we were greeted as usual by the Butler before being ushered into a massive lounge. Surrounded by huge oil paintings, magnificent furniture and solid silver ornaments, we stood transfixed and in awe.

"Blimey," I said, "I bet this lot cost a packet!"

Before my colleague could reply, the door quietly opened and in walked the sister of the deceased.

"Thank you for coming so promptly, but you really needn't have rushed," she said, walking towards a solid-oak mirrored dresser. Opening the drawer, she withdrew from it a small, white paper bag. "I would like you to take this," she said, handing the package to Sister Davies.

"I can't really," spluttered one highly embarrassed nursing Sister.

"But I really must insist," came the rather stern reply, which carried in its tone a hint of annoyance.

"Very well then," said my smiling colleague, delving immediately into the mystery bag.

A look of shock and disbelief now overtook her usual cheerful countenance as she stared down at the article in her hand.

"It's only half empty," said our host. "You must have overlooked it. Will it be of use to another patient?" she said, a quizzical look now adorning her features.

"Yes, yes, zinc and castor oil ointment is always useful," commented a very dazed Sister Davies.

As we drove back to the clinic in silence, I had a sudden idea. "Stop the car," I said.

"What?" she replied.

"Stop the car," I insisted. Pulling up with a screech, she looked at me as if I'd gone mad.

"Give me that pot of ointment," I said. She handed me the offending jar in silence. Getting out of the car I drew my arm back, then with all my might threw the half-full

159

container as far into the distant field as I could. Getting back in the car she looked at me.

"You should bowl for Yorkshire, lad." We stared at one another for a split second before both of us erupted into peals of helpless laughter.

******

Some grim and humorous aspects of the job came to light when, over coffee one afternoon, Sister Davies recounted a few stories from the past.

"There were two eccentric spinster sisters who lived in this run-down old house on the edge of town. They never went out, refused all visitors and had everything they required delivered to the back door. It came as a surprise to the GP, who had seen neither of them for years, when in walked Emily, the younger of the two sisters. She came to request a visit for her sister, Agatha, but would only consider a nurse, no male having ever set foot in their establishment. In fact, if one of them had found the lavatory seat up, it would have caused a mad panic! So the visit was passed onto yours truly, who called the very next morning." Pausing slightly, she gave a shudder. "That day will be etched on my memory for ever."

"Go on," I said, spellbound.

"The house itself was enough to give you the creeps. It could have been used in a horror story: rusty iron gates, unwashed windows, closed dirty brown curtains - it was even thundering when I arrived. After knocking at the front door for what seemed ages, Emily finally let me in, then kept me standing in the hall. The house was absolutely filthy; piles of old newspapers yellow with age stood in heaps everywhere, cobwebs hung from the ceiling and light fittings, and it was so dark you could hardly see. 'Where is Agatha and what's the matter with her?' I enquired. 'She's upstairs in the back bedroom and she can't seem to get out of bed,' replied Emily. 'Right,' I said making for the stairs, 'you coming?' She replied, 'I'll wait down here if you don't mind. The room you want is second on the right. Be careful on the stairs, we have no electricity.'

"Now at this stage I began to feel decidedly uneasy, as I felt my way cautiously upstairs. On reaching the landing, there came a tremendous thunderclap and a flash of lightning which did little to ease my nervousness. I had by now reached the door and opened it slowly. Imagine my relief at seeing, in that darkened room, a little old lady propped up on pillows smiling at me. 'I'm so glad you've come,' she said. 'I can't seem to get out of bed. Can you help me?' It was then that I smelt it: it was vile, and appeared to emanate from the bed. 'Let's take a look see,' I said, gently lifting back the clothes."

Again she paused, giving the by-now familiar shudder

"What did you see?" I asked impatiently.

"The mattress had totally rotted through, all her bodily functions simply falling through onto the floor, but worse was to come! On using my pencil torch I discovered she was not only resting on the iron springs below but was actually impaled on them. She had, to all intents and purposes, become part of the bed!"

"Good God," I said aghast. "What did you do then?"

"Called the GP and the ambulance, then the fire brigade, who managed to extricate her. She was, of course, immediately taken to hospital, where it was discovered that two of the springs had embedded themselves in her buttocks and the wound had turned gangrenous."

"She died, I suppose," I surmised.

"No, surprisingly, she didn't," came the reply. "She was a tough old stick. She even got over a bout of pneumonia, and after her wound had been surgically cleaned and she had undergone a course of antibiotics and vitamin supplements, she made a miraculous recovery."

"Ever been back?" I enquired.

"Good Lord, no," she replied. "They're both dead now!"

Sister Davies also had some rather more humourous stories from the past.

"I had this monthly injection to give of Cytamin or Vitamin B12," she recalled, between sips of coffee. "This old guy always insisted I take away a bag of Brazil nuts after every visit, and very nice they were, too. It was only when I was visiting with a student that the true facts came to light."

"What you mean?" I asked, totally intrigued.

"While I was out of the room, the student remarked how kind it was of the patient to give Sister nuts at each and every visit. 'Yes,' replied the old man. 'I can't stand nuts, but love chocolate, so I suck off the chocolate and give the nuts to Sister. Can't stand waste either!'

"On another occasion I had a first visit, to give a bed bath, and on entering the house, I found the patient lying on the settee. I was in a hell of a rush that day, so quickly filled a bowl at the kitchen sink, grabbed soap, towel and a facecloth and proceeded with the bed bath.

The patient, in his mid-fifties, co-operated well and I soon had him washed and dried, with a clean shirt on. 'There,' I said, 'I bet that feels a lot fresher, doesn't it?' 'Yes,' he replied, 'very nice indeed, but I think it's my father you've come to see. He's upstairs!'"

It was with a sense of regret that I said my goodbyes to Sister Davies. She had treated me with tenderness and a good degree of cheerful tact. Some of the female patients had objected to the presence of a male which I could understand, she made light of it.

"Emily you don't know what you're missing," she said to one old dear.

With a wink she would whisper "Go and sit in the car Mike, put the radio on, there are some sweets in the glove compartment, make the most of it."

She was a lady and a half was Sister Davies.

******

My last and final year appeared to have flown. Once

more I faced the prospect of final exams and these, I discovered, were duplicated on this occasion. There was a hospital final to be taken, plus the state final examinations, once more both written and practical. Miss Grayson explained the reason for this, in what was to be our final block.

"Your hospital finals will be taken first," she said. "If you fail this exam, you will not be eligible for your hospital badge. I would point out that those with high merit marks can obtain either gold, silver or bronze badges."

Later on, seated in my bedroom in Wellgate Mount, I sought the advice from some of the lads.

"It's all a question of luck, really," said Ron. "You either get questions you can answer or questions you can't. It's as simple as that. You can't possibly know everything!"

I could see the sense in what he said, but it didn't really help me much.

"Try and know a little about everything," suggested Dave.

"It's OK for you lot," I said. "You've all recently passed.

"By the way," said Ron, "I'm leaving."

"You're not!" we all said, aghast.

"Yes, I've decided to do mental nursing. It's another eighteen months, but there are better prospects for promotion."

We would all miss Ron, the father figure of the group, but I couldn't blame him. I knew he had been qualified for six years now and had seen student nurses make Sister before him. Matron had at last told him that there was little hope of him becoming a Charge Nurse. There was no fault with him; it was the Consultants - they preferred to have a Sister on their wards. All the other lads were on the lookout, too, for other hospitals up and down the country.

It was with a sense of sadness that I returned to my textbooks after they had left the room. We had become a close-knit group and had shared both good and bad times together. However, change was an inevitable part of life and I had to accept that fact.

As Miss Grayson had predicted, the hospital finals came first as a written paper, then an oral examination. Imagine my horror when I walked into the exam room and was confronted by none other than Mr Charles Parker-Nobbs. If he recognised me, he certainly didn't show it. His face remained expressionless throughout the oral exam.

"What do you think that is?" he said, handing me a small jar in which, suspended in formaldehyde, was a piece of tissue about the size and shape of a child's little finger.

"Is it an appendix, sir?" I said, guessing wildly.

"Are you asking me, or telling me?" came his snapped response.

"I would say it's an appendix," I corrected.

"Yes. What can you tell me about the signs and symptoms of acute appendicitis?" Charles Parker-Nobbs tapped his pen impatiently on the table in front of him, and then glanced at his wristwatch, as he waited for my answer.

"There can be pain, associated nausea and vomiting," I blurted out.

"Could also be a twisted gut, with those symptoms," said Taylor-Nobbs, obviously in no mood to compromise.

"That's true," I replied, "but the pain may be vague at first that is, all over the abdomen, but it usually settles just above the right groin."

"Anything else?" he snapped, looking decidedly bored.

"There is usually guarding and rebound tenderness of the abdomen, and the patient may be pyrexial," I added, looking at him hopefully.

"Right. That will do," he said, scribbling a few remarks on the pad in front of him. With a sinking heart, I left the room. Of all the surgeons in the hospital, I had to cop for him. Ah, well, who needed a hospital badge, anyway?

******

The Final State Examination For The General Part Of The Register followed some three weeks later and this time, on the day in question, I was confronted by a white exam paper. Again, the usual set of instructions that headed the sheet informed me that I had to answer five out of the seven questions set- *On all Aspects of Nursing Care and Treatment of Patients (included in the syllabus of training).*

I decided to attempt answers to the following, in the two and a half hours allowed:-

1) A man of 50 years of age is admitted to hospital with severe chest pain and the diagnosis of coronary thrombosis has been confirmed. Indicate:

a) *the medical treatment which may be given;*

b) *the nursing care which will be necessary,.*

c) *the advice he may be given on discharge from hospital*

3) Write an essay on: "The care of the dying".

4) What can a student nurse learn by visiting patients in their homes with the health visitor or district nurse? Discuss the importance of maintaining links between the hospital and public health nursing services.

6) A man is suspected of having pulmonary tuberculosis.

a) *What investigations may be carried out?*

b) *What drugs will be ordered in the treatment of this condition?*

c) *State what measures may be taken to limit the risk of infecting others, giving reasons.*

7) A child is suffering from acute leukaemia.
a) *What symptoms and signs may be present?*
b) *What medical treatment may be ordered?*
c) *What nursing care will be required?*
d) *What advice and help may be given to anxious relatives?*

I was still writing furiously when time ran out and I was forced to throw down my pen, with a sigh, along with the others. As usual, the whole of the group had decided they had failed as we all split up and went our separate ways. The practical that was the usual formal affair conducted on this occasion by two different Matron Examiners fell lucky with the first who asked me to set up for male catheterisation and bladder irrigation. Not so with the second who decided to test my knowledge of drugs and dosages, ending with the dreaded dilution of lotions question which somehow I managed to stammer my way through.

******

It was some two months later that the results came out. With trembling hands, I opened the buff-coloured envelope bearing my name and exam number. I hardly dared look. I screwed up my eyes and steeled myself for failure.

'Dear Sir,
I have much pleasure in informing you...'

"I've passed. I've passed," I screeched as, along with the rest of the group, we danced and hugged one another in gay abandon.

"Well, Staff Nurse, how does it feel to be a State Registered Nurse?" asked Pat Roebuck, her face positively beaming.

"You tell me," I said. "You should know!"

It was, of course, childish behaviour, but it had been a hard three years and the relief at passing was enormous. I had, much to my surprise, passed the hospital final also, so Charles Parker-Nobbs wasn't such a bad chap, after all! But the culmination of the day for me arrived with a certain telephone call!

"It's someone called Judy for you, Mike," said Tony, handing me the receiver.

"Mike?"

"Yes," I replied, my mouth going suddenly dry.

"Do you remember me?"

"I most certainly do," I replied. "Are you married yet?"

"It's all over, Mike. I've called off the engagement and have applied to train for my SRN at your hospital. I was wondering if that offer of a date still held?"

"Slow down, nurse," said Sister Flint, as I flew passed her. "Is there a fire?"

"Only in my heart, Sister, only in my heart," I said, smiling at her. For a while she stood and watched me, then, slowly shaking her head, she entered theatre, her domain. Odd creatures, these male nurses, she thought, but I suppose they're here to stay!